HIS
CALL
MY ALL

A LESSON IN LOYALTY AND SERVICE

W0017326

KWADWO A. ATTA

FOREWORD BY DR. FRANK OFOSU-APPIAH

His Call My All

Copyright © 2020 by (Kwadwo A. Atta, Aeska Publishing)

kaatta@aeskainc.com

ISBN: 978-1-09835-139-7

Printed in the USA

CONTENTS

ACKNOWLEDGMENTS

In the summer of 1994, you invited me to worship with you at your church in London and to meet your pastor. I didn't really take you seriously, but you insisted. You persisted. You told me I would really like your church and pastor, but I didn't think much of it. I finally agreed after a month to visit your church and meet your pastor. Now twenty-five years later, I'm still enjoying church and faithfully serving under the same pastor you introduced me to. I honor you for being the tool that brought Pastor Frank into my life.

Thank you, Ms. Eva Andoh-Poku (nee Osei-Kweku).

SPECIAL THANKS

To my wife, Eno, you have been my rock of support and comforter for this entire journey. You were there when I learnt all these lessons. You watched me grow and allowed me to serve. Many hours over our weekends and some weekday evenings, you allowed me to go give myself to the things of God in service. For many years when we had no car, you helped me carry instruments from our home, onto public transportation as we did all we could to serve wholeheartedly. You never complained. During the many hours I spent in my study writing deep into the night, you kept encouraging me. I am eternally grateful to you.

To my children, Kaleb and Phoebe, for as long as you've been alive, you have been content sharing me with the world. I missed games and important events, but you did not hold it against me. I have tried to model service and good parenting to you under our circumstances, and it is my prayer that you will serve more than your parents ever did. Service is the key to greatness. Remember that always.

FOREWORD

When it dawned on me that I was being referred to as Kwadwo's Pastor in some circles, I knew that Kwadwo had been noticed as one who holds a special place in the Pastor's heart. Relationships that are God-ordained have many benefits, not only for the people directly involved, but also for the many whose paths they cross. When our paths crossed a quarter of a century ago, little did I know that the relationship would blossom into a destiny defining one that would touch many people's lives all over the world.

I am sure every pastor or leader for that matter dreams or prays for someone who would be sent to hold up their hands in the calling. My prayer was answered, not in the way I envisaged, but in God's own way when He sent Kwadwo to me. As this relationship grew thorough many difficult, trying and also good times in our ministerial formative years in the city of London UK, I began to appreciate it the more. Part of the story of this ongoing journey is told in this book…His Call, My All. However, the real burden of the book is not just the stories and anecdotes, but the lessons one can draw from its pages.

The Principle of Perception tells us that, "Where you sit determines what you see." Over the years, Kwadwo has indeed sat very close to me. He has observed my trials and my triumphs, my pain and my gains; my mountain tops of delight and my dungeons of despair. He has been privileged to observe the good, the bad, the ugly and the in-between of serving in the church. Yet he has maintained a steady course, born out of his relationship with the Savior and an undying resolve to serve no matter what. These observations, experiences and practices have formed the spine of this book. He has lived its message and still does.

In this book, which I strongly recommend to everyone who has been called to serve alongside a leader, Kwadwo forcefully addresses many of the dying virtues that have undergirded service especially in the house of God. Today, loyalty sounds foreign to a generation that lives for its immediate gratification. People get up and leave positions of trust without even a cursory consideration of its implications on others. Many leaders of churches are on the knife-edge of insanity because of the uncertainty of knowing who will hold their hands and be there for the long haul. I have seen pastors quit because they felt all alone, unappreciated and plain burnt out. They had no loyal, dedicated people to hold them up.

We are all hopefully, in agreement that Jesus Christ is the foundation of the Church. However, we should also be mindful of the fact that a foundation by itself would not constitute an edifice. Different building blocks are added to make it a building. You will find such building blocks as you read along. You will be enlightened to the fact that it is not enough just to draw a crowd. To maintain and grow them to become people who serve transcends the numbers game.

To one who may already be serving, this book will put more oil in your tank to go further and serve better. You will discover that some of the things we often overlook can become mighty keys that will help us support our leaders' vision. Dotted in the pages of the book, you will begin to see the importance of proper systems in our churches and organization. You will readily identify with some of the struggles he encountered as he endeavored to build a choir. You will also understand that if you overlook the importance of organizational culture, you will only contribute to your own pain and discomfort.

One great building block that he so strongly emphasizes should be part of any church is the ability to connect. It is very easy for a church to be in a community and yet be anonymous. People will drive from far and near, enjoy some great worship performed by some tired people, hear a great word and leave without the consideration that, that is not the whole essence of church. Every church has a default mandate to be active in their community. There must be innovative ways of doing so without being a nuisance. As you read, endeavor to take note of some of the how-tos.

As he concludes this works, Kwadwo reminds us that serving has an insurance and assurance policy built into it. The Lord certainly looks after those who make it their business to look after His business. There are unquantifiable blessings that follow those who have made His call their all. You will find some of your story in his story and your answers in his answers and your blessings in his blessings.

Read this book prayerfully and live its message fully. Learn your lessons from the lessons taught, and determine to live your life in so much service for your Lord and Master Jesus that when you die and meet Him, He will shake your hand and say to you, I had a blast living in your body. I guess when it happens, and I hope it does, that you will only prostrate before Him and humbly say, you gave me a call, and I gave that call my all.

Dr. Frank Ofosu-Appiah

DEDICATION

To the man I call my father and pastor...
You received me just as I was when I came to you,
young, unshapen, inexperienced, but with a lot of zeal.
You believed in me more than I believed in myself.
You taught me what I needed to negotiate successfully in life.
You encouraged me when the journey got tough.
When I achieved a triumph, you were careful in
how you gave praise because you understood how
that could stop me from being more driven.
When I made the wrong choices, which was often,
you helped me through, sometimes laughing in the
process so that I wouldn't be too hard on myself.
You never forced me to grow up or demanded anything
from me, but in your own special way, you always
created room for me to change for the better.
You gave yourself to many, including me, even when it
cost you more than you could share with others.
You taught me wisdom by asking me how I should deal with certain
situations, even though you already knew the best way to deal with
them. You only wanted to teach me how to think and solve problems.
When I grew up and became a man, you allowed me to
dream and come up with ideas to grow the ministry.
I am reminded daily of a commitment I made in my heart
many years ago, that I will forever seek to be like one of

David's three faithful men, Josheb, Eleazar, and Shammar, who risked their lives to fulfill a whispered wish of King David because they honored, respected, and believed in him. I am a better son, husband, father, and friend because of you.

Papa, I dedicate this book to you.

Medaase.

INTRODUCTION

"Loyalty isn't gray. It's black and white. You're either loyal completely or not loyal at all."

— Sharnay —

I started writing this book not just to memorialize my walk and service under my pastor, but also to discuss some thoughts on loyalty and service as observed through my close walk with a visionary and dynamic man of God. Over many years, my pastor allowed me to walk in the cleft of his leadership as he grew his ministry and influence across the world. I witnessed the hard times, battles, difficulties, betrayals, and where-is-God moments. I saw the many times he would pray for someone to receive an answer to a situation for which he had also been believing God for a long time. Sometimes he would lay hands on the sick when he was carrying much physical pain in his own body, unbeknown to many.

I also witnessed the good times, triumphs, and victories, which were strangely intermingled with the challenging times. I witnessed his fight to see the power of God become a consistent reality and to see the faith and maturity of God's people grow. Every true man or woman of God wrestles with God and men as they work to birth ministry in their members and watch them mature in the basic tenets of our faith. In this book, I want to speak to those who have been called to support a man or woman of God as they establish the call of God on their lives.

Not every faithful servant is called to serve as a pastor of a church. There is a special group of people called to hold the hands of their man or woman of God as they do ministry. To occupy this role, however, is not an easy task. I firmly believe it is a calling, one that requires you to carry the vision of your pastor as if it were your own. It takes wisdom, humility, understanding, and a deep knowledge of service and loyalty. It requires you to be close enough to be a shoulder for your pastor to lean on but removed enough to maintain the reverence and respect of the call on their lives. Achieving that balance takes a lot of wisdom.

There are many examples in the Bible of this type of special relationship between leaders of our faith and ordinary people called to support these leaders: Moses and Joshua, Elijah and Elisha, and David and Jonathan. Many lessons can be gleaned from these relationships as we learn how to support a man or woman of God. I will share some of the valuable lessons I've learned along the way regarding the importance of being loyal and committed to the very end.

I titled this book *His Call My All* to tell my story of how I started serving in church; how I grew in loyalty; and how I came to "own" the vision of my pastor, until his call became my all. It was always a process, starting small but remaining faithful in whatever my pastor committed into my hands. As I proved myself faithful and loyal in the little things, he entrusted more important things to me.

I do not write this book to tout any achievements or elucidate on some profound revelation on loyalty and service. I don't intend to portray myself as unique in any sense, because I know others who have walked this walk and done far better far longer. This is simply my story: observations I have made, things I have come to understand, and lessons I have learned along the journey. I hope to bless someone with what I have learned on this path.

I will also share insights on how to understand your pastor and how to own his or her vision. I will expound on what disposition to adopt when walking close to a pastor and how to maintain reverence when you are exposed to his or her anointing on one side and his or her humanity on the other. It is important to understand the relationship because no matter how you slice it, your pastor is never your friend. He or she should never become someone you banter with or share social media jokes with. I will share the dangers of familiarity and how I determined at all costs to avoid it. This is a determination I made early in ministry and in my walk with my pastor. I understood by revelation that he is my man of God. That title carries an immense burden not to be taken lightly.

Every pastor is in a constant tug of war, stuck in the middle with God on one side and his or her people on the other. Whoever wins this fight directly determines the effectiveness of the pastor's ministry. Having walked with my pastor over the years, I have come to realize that pastoring is a very tough and lonely job. This is why I believe God sends pastors help to enable them to fulfill the call on their lives.

As you read the pages that follow, I pray that you will glean some wisdom that will help position you to serve faithfully in whatever role God has called you to "occupy till I come."

THE ENCOUNTER

People buy into the leader before they buy into the vision.
— John Maxwell —

T his year 2020 marks the twenty-fifth anniversary of my service under Pastor Frank, which began in London, England, and continues to this day in Atlanta, Georgia.

In the summer of 1994, I was vacationing in London as a student from Ghana when a friend of mine, Ms. Eva Andoh-Poku (nee Osei-Kweku) invited me to her church in Deptford, South London. She said I'd love her church and especially her pastor. Of course, I was on vacation in London, having a great time with friends, and not the least bit interested in attending a church service and meeting her pastor. I was already active in my local church in Ghana, but I needed a break from "church folk."

After a long school year, it was common practice for a group of students to travel to London during the summer months, with two goals in mind: to make as much money as possible doing odd jobs and then to have as much fun as possible. Nothing else mattered. But that year was different because the educational system in Ghana had ground to a halt due to a teacher strike. At some point, I planned to transfer to London to continue my education if this uncertainty prevailed.

Though a Christian at the time, I certainly was not interested in mixing my fairly short holiday with any church activities. Fact is, I needed a break, but Ms. Eva gently persisted as only she could do. So, one Sunday in the summer of 1994, I decided to follow her to Living Springs International Church, just to get her off my. It was a quaint little hall that doubled as a basketball court right next to a busy market. The building in which the church was located was called the Shaftesbury Christian Center. It was a medium-sized church, and everyone I met appeared to enjoy being there. That certainly caught my attention. I attended the main service, hoping to have the experience Ms. Eva had been raving about.

I remember the service like it was yesterday. I was blown away by the simplicity of the pastor yet the profound wisdom that exuded from the pulpit. He spoke with such eloquence and power that I was transfixed. Suddenly, I began to look forward to meeting him in person.

After the service, I stood by the side of the hall, waiting for Ms. Eva to formally introduce me to her pastor, who had just blown my mind with a forty-five-minute message. I observed him walking around the hall as many gathered to say hello to him. He came across as a very genuine, down-to-earth young man who was highly focused on building the church he led. He spoke the word of God with such clarity and wisdom, intriguing me from day one.

"My name is Frank," he said as he introduced himself to me with a smile, warmth, and a strong handshake. He welcomed me and said he was very happy to have me visit the church and he hoped to see me again. A very simple but profound encounter in many ways, but I left knowing I had been affected in a strange and powerful way. I remember giving Ms. Eva a thumbs-up for inviting me to her church. I enjoyed it greatly. Little did I know, this was the beginning of an incredible journey.

THE BEGINNING

As fate would have it, the impasse in the Ghanaian educational system prevailed and I decided to find a school to attend in London. I did this knowing that living on my own in London, away from my norm, was going to be a challenge. I knew London quite well from a short-stay or vacation perspective, but it is always daunting to move to a new environment to start living a new life. I also knew I was going to have to fend for myself with little to no family support, but I still transferred schools and started my civil engineering education at the University of Westminster.

After my first visit to the church, I kept visiting every week while convincing myself to make it my home church. One day after the service, Pastor Frank walked up to me to say hello, which was his usual practice. He thanked me for continuing to visit the church and asked me how I could help grow the vision through service. At the time, I was a musician and had successfully started a dynamic choir in Ghana prior to moving to London. I told him I was a bass guitarist and gave him a brief summary of my experience. I then offered to help with his music team. He looked at me and said, "Come and let's work together." He asked me to build a choir in the church since they had only a small praise team.

I was twenty-two years old with little experience in building a music program, but he still trusted me with starting the choir. I used to wonder what he saw in me that made him trust me with such a major project. I had been around choirs for some time, so I had some idea of how difficult it is to build one. I knew one fact that it was a no-fun job and it certainly made me rethink his request.

I went home that day with my mind laden with thoughts about what I had just been asked to do. Of course, I knew music to an appreciable extent, but I had never taught a choir. That is a totally different proposition. In Ghana I was responsible for leading the choir I formed as the manager, but not for teaching parts and harmonies. So obviously, I was concerned about what I was getting into.

THE DEFINING MOMENT

After I got home, I went quietly to my room and prayed about this role I had been asked to occupy. I had to know not only how to teach music, but also how to work with and lead people, most of whom would probably be older than I was. The next day, still in deep thought with a lot of apprehension, I stood by my window in my room and looked across the apartment complex, which was located at the corner of A205 and Kings Avenue in Clapham South, London.

As I was standing there, my eyes became fixed on one of the units in the block across from mine, about 500 feet away. A short time later, a man with a bowl in his hands came and stood on the balcony of his second-floor apartment. After standing there for a few seconds, he threw the contents of the bowl across the lawn. Multiple wood pigeons suddenly flew in to enjoy this feast they were apparently not expecting. At that moment, I heard a voice clearly tell me that if I would commit to service in the house of God and do what my pastor had asked me to do, God would take complete control over my needs. The voice said I would never have to worry about my needs if I gave myself and whole-heartedly served. It was a stunning moment because I heard it clearly. In fact, I had to turn to make sure no one was behind me, that I really was alone in my room.

Throughout the Bible, we see evidence of the importance of tying our commitments to God to a personal encounter. I had obviously just had mine, but little did I know it was going to steer my life in ministry forevermore. The wood pigeons are regularly seen all over London, so it was common to see them swarm over the crumbs the gentleman threw on the lawn, even though they were nowhere to be seen prior.

The timing of it, however, combined with the context of my thoughts and the voice I heard, made it a defining moment for me.

Then Matthew 6:26 came to mind:

> "Look at the birds. They don't plant or harvest or store food in barns, for your heavenly Father feeds them. And aren't you far more valuable to Him than they are?" (Matthew 6:26, NKJV)

That scripture struck a chord in my heart and gave me peace about what I was contemplating. I also knew that once I started down the path the pastor had asked me to travel, I couldn't look back. So, I did all I could to count the cost of building a choir from scratch in a new city with a new culture.

I decided to read all of Matthew 6. It is hard for me to accurately articulate what happened in my heart as I read it.

> "Now if God so clothes the grass of the field, which today is, and tomorrow is thrown into the oven, will He not much more clothe you, O you of little faith? Therefore, do not worry, saying, 'What shall we eat?' or 'What shall we drink?' or 'What shall we wear?' For after all these things the Gentiles seek. For your heavenly Father knows that you need all these things. But seek first the kingdom of God and His righteousness, and all these things shall be added to you." (Matthew 6:30-33, NKJV)

The Message translation shows how awesome this Scripture is:

> "If God gives such attention to the appearance of wild-flowers—most of which are never even seen—don't you think He'll attend to you, take pride in you, do His

best for you? What I'm trying to do here is to get you to relax, to not be so preoccupied with getting, so you can respond to God's giving. People who don't know God and the way He works fuss over these things, but you know both God and how he works. Steep your life in God-reality, God-initiative, God-provisions. Don't worry about missing out. You'll find all your everyday human concerns will be met. (Matthew 6:30-33, MSG)

I was sold! On that day, I locked myself into a covenant with God and made a commitment to serve with all my heart, with the earnest expectation that this scripture would be fulfilled in my life.

UNDERSTAND THE CALL

God does not choose people because of their
ability, but because of their availability.

— *Brother Andrew* —

The whisperings of purpose and destiny always resound in the ears of those called for an assignment. If you listen hard enough, you will hear the sound. Over the years, many people have asked me how I came to know that I was called to serve my pastor in his ministry, and my response is always that there was a witness within me that I was called to serve under him. It has always been clear to me from the time I met him, but having the witness within me was the first step. When I first met and interacted with my pastor and perceived he was a good man who loved to see nothing but God glorified, I knew I was onto a good thing. I knew I had found someone I could follow and look up to. I had to make the choice to serve wholeheartedly regardless of the cost. For those of you called to support your pastor and his or her vision, this chapter is for you.

The Bible tells the story of the transfiguration of Jesus on the Mount:

> And He said unto them, Verily I say unto you, that there
> be some of them that stand here, which shall not taste
> of death, till they have seen the kingdom of God come
> with power. And after six days Jesus taketh with him

Peter, and James, and John, and leadeth them up into a high mountain apart by themselves: and He was transfigured before them. And His raiment became shining, exceeding white as snow; so as no fuller on earth can white them. And there appeared unto them Elias with Moses: and they were talking with Jesus. And Peter answered and said to Jesus, Master, it is good for us to be here: and let us make three tabernacles; one for thee, and one for Moses, and one for Elias. For He wist not what to say; for they were sore afraid. And there was a cloud that overshadowed them: and a voice came out of the cloud, saying, This is my beloved Son: hear him. And suddenly, when they had looked round about, they saw no man anymore, save Jesus only with themselves. (Mark 9:1-8, KJV)

The King James Version of this scripture gives a lot of insight into the call God confers on some people to support visionaries in accomplishing a major purpose for the Kingdom. It is, however, a scripture that many contend with since it appears to say that some of the disciples standing in front of Jesus would not die until they witness the Kingdom of God come in power. I used to struggle with this scripture as well until my understanding grew with time. The account details Jesus choosing three of His disciples who were called and *taking* them up a mountain *apart* by themselves on another journey where they witnessed a glorious, but frightening, revelation of who Jesus really is in all His glory. While many were called to be with Jesus, He chose only a few to go to another level of revelation with Him.

> The whisperings of purpose and destiny always resound in the ears of those called for an assignment

Many have questioned why Jesus chose those three, and indeed it is a question worth asking. Some have said they were chosen because they were closest to the Master, while others have said it was because of the specific task He had for them after His departure. But whatever the reasons were, we do know the Lord was pleased to choose them and take them on a different journey to reveal His honor and glory to them. The experience for the three chosen ones was going to leave an indelible mark on them for the rest of their lives.

Many times, walking with a true man or woman of God can be a frightening experience when we see God working through him or her. I had a jaw-dropping experience the first time I got to travel with my pastor on a mission trip to Amsterdam. He had been invited to minister at a friend's church. By that point, I had been serving under him for a couple of years in London, seeing him do his usual effective ministry weekly. However, this experience of traveling with him to minister outside of our church was anything but ordinary. I felt like I was seeing him minister like a different man. He moved in power and I saw many delivered and set free like I had never witnessed before. I was almost terrified of what I saw him do on that trip. Things were happening all over the church building the program was being hosted in, as many had a real encounter with God through my pastor's ministry. I felt privileged to have had that experience. I remember him looking at me with a smile on his face after the church service and asking me why I looked so terrified. I had seen the glory of God work so freely in a man I thought I knew, who was transformed into a different man. Of course, I had the privilege of having subsequent similar experiences with him as I continued to walk with him.

On another occasion, I visited my pastor in his home to have a discussion regarding a certain matter. At the end of the meeting, he sent me to pick up something for him from his bedroom. This was my first time going into his bedroom. When I got to the door, I walked in, picked up the item he asked me to find, and went downstairs where he and the first lady were. I left the house not long after this and went home. When I got home later that day, I started feeling troubled, as if I had done something wrong. It was a weird feeling that I could not understand. I tried to make sense of this uneasiness within me, but nothing made sense. Later that night, as I lay down to sleep, the unrest got worse and I certainly got worried. Then, as time went on, I saw an image of my feet walking into my pastor's room with my shoes on.

As I tried to make sense of that image in my spirit, it got even more vivid. All I saw was my feet walking into his bedroom, in the exact shoes I had worn that morning. Then it hit me that the unrest was all about the fact that I had casually walked into my pastor's bedroom as if it were my own, with my shoes on. A few moments after I saw this image in my head and understood it to mean the casual nature with which I had walked in my pastor's room, the uneasy feeling left me. It felt as though a weight had been lifted off my shoulders. That experience will be with me as long as I live. I said nothing of this to my pastor, but I got the message loud and clear.

I did not interpret this experience to mean simply not wearing shoes into his bedroom; there was bigger message—*to never get familiar with my pastor.* Your pastor is chosen by God to fulfil a very important assignment on Earth, and it is important that you always keep this understanding within you. Subsequent to that experience, anytime he's asked me to do something in his bedroom, I take my shoes off and walk in backward. I haven't had that strange, uneasy experience since I started doing that.

Now, I am not suggesting that everyone do exactly what I did. This was a personal experience, unique to my own relationship with my pastor, which I believe God used to teach me something about my close walk with him. Choosing to take my shoes off and walk into his bedroom backward anytime he has asked me to pick up anything or take something to his room was part of my effort to ensure I revere my pastor as my man of God.

THE PAIN OF BEING CHOSEN

Being chosen can often feel like being pulled apart. Jesus chose the three disciples to be by themselves with Him. Many of you working in

God's vineyard can testify to this feeling of dealing with the honor of being called while you're dealing with your humanity, struggles, fears, uncertainties, insecurities, and weaknesses. This can often feel like being pulled apart. People with a strong calling on their lives are always pulled apart, often without being able to understand that feeling.

Being called can be a lonely experience. Even when I was a young boy, I felt as though I did not fit in. I tried to fit in and feel accepted in school, but it always felt as though I had to put forth a big effort. Many people I met treated me different from others, as though they did not want to allow me within their circles to do the normal things others could do with them. Other people treated me with some kind of strange reverence and respect that seemed to make them uncomfortable to be around me. As a result, I felt very lonely, trying to understand why I did not fit in.

I was almost convinced there was something wrong with me. I felt like a square peg in a round hole. I did not realize God had a specific call for me that required separation. So, I did things to try to circumnavigate what I thought was an anomaly in an effort to fit in. But the more I tried, the less successful I was. For many years, I did not understand it, and it was a constant struggle within. But after a while, I just decided to accept myself, no matter how different or alone I felt. Period.

Even though I did not get this early enough, it was important for me to understand the unique path God had called me to walk required that I not be flippant and careless about who I chose to associate with. I wish I had understood this much earlier in life but thank God it's never too late to make a change. Many of you are either going through this experience I have just described or have already been through it. You feel different and many times alone in your interactions with others. Sometimes even the people

> The honor of being called and the dichotomy of dealing with your humanity, struggles, fears, uncertainties, insecurities, and weaknesses, can often feel like being pulled apart.

surrounding you in church don't seem to get you. I want you to know that God may be trying to get your attention, to teach you some important lessons about what He has called you to be and to do.

It is believed that Mount Hermon, where Jesus was transfigured, is about 9,200 feet high. That is almost two miles high, assuming He and the three disciples went all the way to the top. If you have walked up a mountain before, you know how the weather can change on your way up. At that time of the year, it was bound to be super cold at the summit, but much warmer on the ground. As they went up, they would have expected the weather to change, requiring them to constantly adapt to the changing environment around them as they followed their man of God.

I once vacationed in Hawaii and stayed on the Island of Maui. One of the major attractions of this beautiful island is Mount Haleakala, which is about 10,000 feet high, not much higher than Mount Hermon. It is known to have one of the best views of a sunrise if you are able to make it to the top of the mountain before dawn...and that's about 5:30 a.m. I decided to try and witness this majestic view I had heard so much about, and nothing was going to hold me back. Little did I know how difficult going up the mountain in the darkness would be. I am not necessarily a fan of heights.

On the day I decided to drive up the mountain with my wife, it was 70° F on the ground, even at 2:00 a.m. I wonder what she was thinking at the time, probably something like *Could you love me a little bit less?* As we set off on this three-hour trip, the weather got colder and the road narrower as we got higher up the mountain. As we began negotiating sharp bends and inclines, we wondered whether we had made the right decision to go up the mountain at that time of the night. It was very dark outside as you would expect it to be. But we didn't give up and eventually made it up the steep, windy, and fairly narrow road to the top in a little over three hours. The temperature was below freezing, and we had to bundle up with multiple blankets, which we carried along with us. It's not easy to find a winter jacket in Hawaii at any time of the year. There was about a 70° difference in temperature between the ground and the mountaintop. We arrived just in time to stand at the edge of the mountain, some 4,000 feet above the thick clouds below us, and watch the sun spew these awesome colors across the horizon as it rose in majesty. It's an experience I will never forget. The view was so spectacular that it made the entire difficult journey up the mountain worthwhile.

Many times, being called is exactly like this. You go on a journey by yourself, through difficult terrain, winding roads, and changing temperatures to a destination you don't even know about. During this journey, you have multiple opportunities to turn back and return to familiar territory, and all the while you're wondering why you even had to go on this trip in the first place. My entire trip up Mount Haleakala was in uncomfortable and unfamiliar territory. It was even scary and lonely most of the time because I thought something terrible was going to happen. But driving up the many narrow and winding roads, I had to let the reward of the endeavor overrule the pull of the familiar if I was going to be able to count myself among those who had made it to the top. Until you come to the place where the revelation and reward of what you do outweighs the reality and the difficulty of the effort required, you will always have an opportunity to quit.

This experience gives me a fairly good picture of what the chosen disciples experienced, although what they witnessed at the top was far more glorious and incomparable to what I saw. They followed their master willingly and wholeheartedly, not knowing where they were headed, or how treacherous the walk up was going to be. They were responsive to their master's call, and they followed Jesus at a moment's notice, without even hesitating. They were sold out to their master. No one complained about the

> Until you come to the place where the revelation and reward of what you do outweighs the reality and the difficulty of the effort required, you will always have an opportunity to quit.

cold or the difficult terrain they were on, nor showed concern about the destination. They simply followed their pastor. That is true servanthood.

When you are chosen to serve in any capacity, especially under your pastor directly, it is often a difficult, but rewarding, experience. You contend with the upward pull of your call as well as the downward pull of your inconsistencies. You doubt yourself often, and you will fight what I call the "battle of man." You will learn to deal with people whose attitudes and character come in all shapes and sizes. Many will try to define you from their own limited lens. You have to sacrifice your time and many things that mean a lot to you in order to stay focused and remain relevant in your service. It is part of the process, which is rigorous and dependent upon your obedience, but it is needful.

I was blessed to know early in my walk with my pastor that I had been called to serve under him. Once I made the connection that he was the one God had called me to serve, and that his church is where God had called me to serve, the rest became easy. Nothing that came my way was strong enough to get me to walk away and quit. While I did face many struggles and disappointments, I kept holding on in service. I received some awesome opportunities to move away and pursue my career goals in other cities, but I gave those up so I could stay in my role in church. For some reason, I knew without a shadow of doubt that every sacrifice I made was directly linked to my upward progress in my life and career. I remembered my initial encounter and covenant always. I made up my mind that nothing was going to move me away from what I had been called to do. I had no backup plan. Was the journey in service difficult? Absolutely. Did I feel like giving up? Often. Did I make mistakes? Multiple times. Did I always agree with my pastor's decisions? Certainly not. But I kept my focus on being present to serve and take care of whatever had been entrusted into my hands.

PROCESS AND TOLERANCE

You can never fully and effectively be used by God if you have not been processed.

Church is a hospital in many respects, with a lot of people who are imperfect and under construction entrusted with handling the holy things of God. In the Bible, there's no shortage of error-prone people being processed and used by God for the establishment of His purpose. God never called a perfect church but is intent on seeing us grow to maturity to handle the deeper things of God. God can never fully and effectively use you if you have not gone through the process of development to a state of maturity and trust as a true, dependable servant. One of my favorite scriptures about process is found in Jeremiah 18:4 (AMP):

> And the vessel that he was making from clay was spoiled in the hand of the potter; so he made it over, reworking it into another vessel as it seemed good to the potter to make it.

At any particular time, we are going through some stage of processing from marred clay to one that seems good to the Potter. This is a personal but necessary process for all of us so we can become the workmen who rightly handle the word of Truth. Having been an intent observer of all things church, I painfully realize this is where we lose a lot of our people. The church can be so merciless and intolerant of those in development that we force some to leave just because they don't fit the mold others have set for them. As a result, we are losing people in the middle of their development because of merciless people who identify themselves with a merciful God. It's baffling. There are

Suit up and jump on the center court to advance the Kingdom. Do not suspend your ministry development by choosing to sit on the bleachers and point out how others ought to run and fight.

not many other entrenched rumor mills than those we find in some of our churches today. Too many among us just seem to thrive and feed off the errors of others. I don't even waste my time listening to stories about people's failures. I could care less. What's the glory in gloating over others when they make a mistake or don't seem to measure up to the standard that you have set for them in your mind? . Why would I make someone's failure a source of conversation or laughter for me? Who made me a judge over another? Why would we hurt some so deeply that they end up leaving the church that accepted all of us in the first place? What do we gain by doing that? Everyone we meet in church is like the clay depicted in Jeremiah 18:4, at a different stage of development in their walks with God. Of course, our obedience and understanding feed very much into how long our processing takes, but I want to throw some light on this, so we develop some tolerance for each other.

People who have not been processed do not have mercy, nor do they understand their own limitations. This makes them unequipped for the journey they have been asked to embark on in support of a vision. So instead of being on the center courts, helping to advance the kingdom, they suspend their development, choose to sit on the bleachers, and point out how others ought to run and fight. One of my absolute best quotations is by Theodore Roosevelt. He said:

> "It is not the critic who counts; not the man who points out how the strong man stumbles, or where the doer of deeds could have done them better. The credit belongs to the man who is actually in the arena, whose face is marred by dust and sweat and blood, who strives valiantly; who errs and comes short again and again; because there is not effort without error and shortcomings;"

Criticism is cheap and anyone can afford to criticize. The credit and praise never goes to those who sat by to criticize those who have rolled up their sleeves to work regardless of their faults.

People who have not been processed can be hypocritical, dishonest about their own failings, and experts at being critical of others. They choose to magnify and gloat the mistakes of others who have submitted themselves to God to be processed for service. God cannot use you if you have not received with meekness the implanted word, which is able to save your soul and help process you.

Throughout the Bible, we see multiple examples of those who had to face their own limitations and failures during their journeys and walks with God. God allowed and still allows His servants to go through situations because He knows they will come out better on the other side. I remember when Peter flat out denied knowing Jesus, even though just a few hours prior, he had categorically rejected the idea that he ever would deny Jesus even though Jesus gave him foreknowledge of his impending failure.

> Along the way Jesus said to them, "Before the night is over, you will all desert me. This will fulfill the prophecy of the Scripture that says: I will strike down the shepherd and all the sheep will scatter far and wide! "But after I am risen, I will go ahead of you to Galilee and will meet you there." Then Peter spoke up and said, "Even if all the rest lose their faith and fall away, I will still be beside you, Jesus!" Are you sure, Peter?" Jesus said. "In fact, before the rooster crows a few hours from now, you will have denied me three times." Peter replied, "I absolutely will never deny you, even if I have to die with you!" And all the others said the same thing. (Matthew 26:31-35, TPT)

> Meanwhile, Peter was still sitting outside in the courtyard when a servant girl came up to him and said, "I recognize you. You were with Jesus the Galilean." In front of everyone Peter denied it and said, "I don't have a clue

what you're talking about." Later, as he stood near the gateway of the courtyard, another servant girl noticed him and said, "I know this man is a follower of Jesus the Nazarene!" Once again, Peter denied it, and with an oath he said, "I tell you, I don't know the man!" A short time later, those standing nearby approached Peter and said, "We know you're one of his disciples—we can tell by your speech. Your Galilean accent gives you away!"

Peter denied it, and using profanity he said, "I don't know the man!" At that very moment the sound of a crowing rooster pierced the night. Then Peter remembered the prophecy of Jesus, "Before the rooster crows you will have denied me three times." With a shattered heart, Peter went out of the courtyard, sobbing with bitter tears. (Matthew 26:69-75, TPT)

Take a look at Peter's encounter with himself. Here was a man who had been handpicked by God to lead the church after Jesus's departure, vehemently deny knowing Jesus as His persecution and trial unfolded that night. Only earlier that evening had Jesus said to His disciples that "one of you will deny me...."

Peter replied, "I absolutely will never deny you, even if I have to die with you!" And all the others said the same thing.

Fast forward a couple of hours into the night, and there he was, swearing he didn't know Jesus. In fact, he denied Jesus three times in succession before the cock crowed as Jesus turned to look at him. When he remembered the prophecy Jesus had given him, he ran out of the courtyard and wept bitterly.

Peter did not know himself, so he was quick to make a bold statement that he would never deny Jesus. I have no doubt he meant what he said, but he made the promise without a full appreciation of his own limitations. This is probably one of the most painful experiences of the

Bible because a trusted servant denied his own master during his hour of need. It was necessary for him to go through that process, however, because Jesus had said of Peter, "you are Peter, and on this rock I will build my church, and the gates of hell will not prevail against it." This is the promise and purpose God had for the man who was subsequently going to deny Him, yet He still chose to use him. Who among them could have guessed what God had in store for Peter?

Peter's denial of Jesus was not a deviation from the purpose of God, but part of the process necessary to get Peter ready for what lay ahead. It is important to realize this so you do not mischaracterize your failings and those of others. Peter had to be processed out of what he did not even know was in him. The Potter had to rework his clay to form a vessel that was fit for His use. Can you imagine the torment he went through when he realized he had denied Jesus in His time of need? Can you imagine the disappointment he felt? He saw Jesus, whom he loved so much, being beaten, harassed, tormented, and killed and he swore he didn't know Him. I don't know if any rumors circulated about how Peter had denied Jesus in the run up to His crucifixion, but if some of the "church people" I see now were there, I would not be surprised. Imagine the anguish he felt as the night went on and he observed his "pastor" being nailed to the cross. Imagine the pain he felt knowing he wasn't there when his "pastor" needed him the most.

> Peter's denial of Jesus was not a deviation from the purpose of God but part of the process necessary to get Peter ready for what lay ahead.

Funny enough, there was probably not much difference between Peter and Judas if you examine their actions critically. One betrayed Jesus, and the other denied Him. One told the enemy "I know Him, and here is where you can find Him," and the other said, "I don't know Him." Both were part of Jesus's inner circle, but was either better off than the other? Not until we see their responses. One ran off and committed suicide, while the other ran off to confront his error and hope Jesus would restore him, which He did.

> "Peter, my dear friend, listen to what I'm about to tell you. Satan has demanded to come and sift you like wheat and test your faith. But I have prayed for you, Peter, that you would stay faithful to me no matter what comes. Remember this: after you have turned back to me and have been restored, make it your life mission to strengthen the faith of your brothers." (Luke 22:31-22, NKJV)

Earlier, Peter had also received this prophecy, which may have strengthened him when he failed. Peter was so important to Jesus that after He rose from the dead and announced His resurrection to the disciples, he said:

> "...Go tell my disciples and PETER..."
> (Mark 16:7, NIV)

Jesus knew Peter was tormenting himself, and He wanted him to know He still loved him in spite of the fact that he had denied knowing Him. So, He sent Peter a personal message: "Go tell Peter that I am alive." How refreshing this message must have been for him. Imagine being in Peter's shoes. He was so discouraged that he even went back to fishing. Failure has a way of making us give up everything we've worked hard for. His failure may have made him forget or give up on all the wonderful prophecies Jesus had given him. But Jesus never forgot him. He died thinking about Peter and rose with Peter on His mind. When Jesus had restored him, the Bible tells of the impact he had building the church after Jesus was taken up into heaven. He could not have done that without being processed. He had to go through the fire in order to be made ready for what lay ahead.

In my own life and ministry, I have made multiple mistakes. Like Paul, my own behavior has often baffled me. I have gone through doubt, pain, scandal, and shame, due to my own choices, bad judgment, and, of course, just plain gossip. But I did not allow myself to quit the ministry because of it. I kept pressing on and making myself available for Jesus to use me. People have talked about me during my times of trial. Many times, it was those I trusted and looked up to who let me down the most. I was, however, determined enough to keep pressing on and not listen to the self-appointed judges who gloat on the apparent failures of those trying to be better vessels for the Master's use. If I had not been processed and gone through tough times, who knows where I would be now?

Now I understand the failings of people. I did not know then that I would now be sitting in a place where I have the responsibility of helping to flesh out the vision of restoration in our church and help my pastor grow a ministry where this vision is a reality. If I had refused to go through my processing and allowed pride to get the better of me when I was shunned, mischaracterized, and misrepresented, I would have walked away and separated myself from a more fulfilling future and destiny.

> Be careful what you promise and what you think you would never do. Peter said, "I would never deny you!"

In your day of strength, be careful what you promise and what you think you would never do. Peter said "I would never do that..." because he thought he knew himself. He believed in himself and his accomplishments because he had not failed yet. He was the first of the disciples to have a revelation that Jesus was the son of the living God. He was an accomplished fisherman who had a business. He was sold out to Jesus and not afraid to stand for Him. He took out a sword and struck off one of the ears of the soldiers who came to arrest Him. When Jesus came to them, walking on the water, it was Peter who stepped off the boat to walk on water as the others stayed in the boat. No doubt he was accomplished on all accounts. But sometimes continued success can make you think you are invulnerable and can't fail. This is why the Bible cautions us, "So beware if you think it could never happen to you, lest your pride becomes your downfall." (1 Corinthians 10:12 TPT)

For those of you called to serve or walk beside your pastor, be careful how you categorize others within the fold of the ministry. Even the disruptive and proud person on your team can be part of God's plan. Do not be quick to write people off because you never know what God has for each person you encounter. Jesus told us to allow the wheat and the tares to grow together, for everyone is in a different state of processing. One of the biggest mistakes we can make is to judge others from the perspective of where we stand. The mere fact that you would not do something does not mean you are perfect. I have seen people come into our ministry, gifted and available, but with a wrong attitude. There have been some that my pastor has allowed to come close that I have had doubts about. Yet, when I remember these examples above, I recognize that God can use anyone and is still working on everyone, including me! Always remember that God is working on everyone and allow them to go through their process and development. Some may stay in the oven a bit longer than others, but that doesn't make them bad people. If my pastor had given up on me when I was making dumb decisions, where would I be today?

UNDERSTAND YOUR PASTOR'S HEART

I have come to accept that my pastor's heart is almost unreal. I sometimes find myself wondering how he manages to do have such a heart for people. Your pastor's heart is what makes him or her tick. It is who he or she is, and until you understand his or her heart, you won't understand the vision he or she carries. The vision for All Nations Church, led by my pastor, is as follows:

"Restoring people and releasing their potential by connecting them to Christ."

If I were visiting our church and had the opportunity to connect
with the pastor for longer than thirty minutes, and I was asked to guess
what his vision is, I would at least have gotten the restoration part right.
During my early years with Pastor Frank, he shared his heart with me
and talked about the burden God had placed on him to restore the
broken and let them find the strength to live again. He said, "People
are hurting...." At the time, I did not fully grasp what he meant by that
statement, but over time, I understood. One of his famous statements
is the "church is a hospital, and sick people go there to find wellness...."
This has characterized his ministry for as long as I have been with him.
I have seen him open his heart to many and help them on this journey
called life. This is what makes him tick, helping people find the strength
to live again.

If you are called to serve under a pastor, you have to understand
his or her heart. The heart of a pastor fuels his or her drive for what he
or she is pursuing. It helps you understand why pastors do what they
do, because you can get quite confused when you try to understand
certain actions they take or decisions they make. Understanding who
your pastor is and what drives him or her is crucial if you're going to
have a mutually beneficial and successful relationship. Two cannot walk
together unless they agree, as the scriptures have so eloquently stated.

"Can two walk together, unless they are agreed?" (Amos
3:3, NKJV)

Amos 3:3 says two cannot walk together unless they have a common
understanding and acceptance of their walk toward the fulfilment of a
vision. I cannot serve faithfully under my pastor if I do not understand,
accept, and share his heart for people.

UNDERSTAND THE VISION

The heart of your pastor is directly connected to his or her vision. You have to understand and own the vision he or she aspires to if you are going to be an advocate and ladder holder. To own a vision means you are totally sold out to supporting it in any way that helps achieve it. So, if I believe in my pastor's heart for restoration, then I have to have a heart for people. If my pastor goes all out to love and protect people regardless of their failures, then I can't walk with him if I have a heart that is critical of others.

As a church, we have constantly communicated our vision. We have advertised it daily through infomercials and other platforms to constantly remind our people why we gather and where we are headed. This is an effort to create an awareness and obtain subsequent buy-in from those called to support the vision. A vision describes what an organization needs to be like to be deemed successful in the future. When I am invited to speak to leaders and volunteers at other churches on how they can achieve their vision, I typically pass out Post-It notes and ask everyone to anonymously write down the vision of their church and pass it back to me. To date, the best I have seen is about two out of every ten people get it right. That's only 20 percent. Other times, I throw out random statements like, "Our leadership team is in agreement on the vision and the strategy to achieve it," and ask audience members to write their opinions of it. It's always amazing to me the disparity in responses I get.

Every organization has a responsibility to make the vision plain and known, and those of us who serve have an even greater responsibility to know it, own it and run with it. Vision is what should inform our choices and feed our passion. If the people you lead don't know or understand your vision, they won't be with you for the long haul. It is paramount that you explain the vision to your church or organization consistently so you can obtain buy-in from your members.

Earlier I shared the vision of restoration for our church, which means having a heart for people. It implies the need for me to go out of my way to care for and be tolerant and nonjudgmental of everyone God sends my way because everyone has a story. One famous saying I have encountered in my readings is, "Don't judge a man until you have walked two moons in his moccasins." I love that statement. Everyone needs some help now and then, and the fact that a person needs help in a specific area does not make that person bad.

> Every organization has a responsibility to make the vision plain and known, and those of us who serve have an even greater responsibility to know it, own it and run with it.

Everyone you encounter is, for the most part, a product of their own choices and the circumstances they grew up in. With time, I understood it was important for me to grow to become the person who helps pull people through their battles. I had to become a load bearer, not only for my pastor, but also for those God blessed our ministry with. I have had to exemplify the characteristics that embody the vision I profess to believe in and support. This is especially important for those called to directly support a pastor on this journey.

Dr. Gary Fenton, senior pastor of Dawson Memorial Baptist Church in Birmingham, Alabama, made the following statement:

> "...when you understand your pastor's vision, you can shape the vision of your own ministry to support the bigger-picture goals. It will be much easier to gain the mindshare of your senior pastor when you can speak his language."

This is a solid statement of truth. You have to understand your pastor's vision and then shape your personal vision to support the bigger vision because it's about something bigger than you. It is absolutely pertinent to get on the same wavelength as your pastor to demonstrate that you understand and have a passion for the vision. When people are misaligned with the pastor and the vision, they run wild and do things out of alignment. Some even leave out of rebellion under the guise of a calling to set up their own ministries.

I have seen gifted people called to support visionaries run off to start their own ministry because they could not submit to another. They did not understand that together they could achieve more. Of course, I am not opposed to people starting their own ministries as long as they preach the word and bring people into the kingdom. But they have to move with God and be in step with His plans. It is a dangerous thing to move ahead of God and set up churches to become the "guardians" of people's souls. This is the greatest and most humbling experience, so please do not rush into it. I have seen some pastors struggle to get beyond the initial startup phase of their churches because maybe, they're not doing what God called them to do with the right heart, motive or per God's timing.

YOU ARE NOT CALLED TO FIGHT YOUR PASTOR'S BATTLES

Your job in supporting your pastor is to be fully focused on carrying the vision and keeping its wheels turning regardless of what is going on. By virtue of the role your pastor occupies, he or she will fight many battles, both spiritually and physically, as he or she tries to lead the flock and the organization. Some will love your pastor, and others will hate, talk about, or betray him or her. But when people let your pastor down, it is not your job to internalize those emotions and retaliate against those who have caused your pastor emotional harm. I am not saying you must be friends with them and banter with them, but do not use your role to become polarized toward certain individuals, or that emotion will begin to inform your decisions and your thinking. The Bible instructs us to watch over our hearts with all diligence, for everything we do flows from it.

When you are sold out to your pastor and his or her vision, your heart and mind are committed to someone and something you esteem, cherish, and pledge allegiance to. If you are close to your pastor, you will see certain things the ordinary person will not see. You will be exposed to some of the betrayals and hurts your pastor experiences, and it is easy to carry them and respond to them as if they were your own. But if you are not careful, you will become like Peter in the Garden when the soldiers came with Judas to arrest Jesus. He immediately took out his sword and cut off one of the soldier's ears. But immediately after, Jesus took the ear and ministered healing to the enemy, right in front of Peter.

I used to carry my pastor's emotional disappointments too. I would get upset at those who hurt my pastor and erase their relevance from my domain. I would run off on an emotional tangent and become their enemy. But many times, I would see my pastor forgive and reconnect with those same people and accept them back home like the father of the prodigal son, all the while I was fighting the same emotions the older brother exhibited. My pastor certainly has a special grace that enables him to love even those who have hurt him. I am also painfully aware that I do not share that same grace. I have realized the best strategy is never to fight those battles but to remain focused on being a support and an ear for my pastor so that I don't become distracted with anger and disappointment. My untainted counsel and listening ear are more important than my sword. I am not necessarily suggesting you remain cordial and break bread with people who have hurt you or your pastor, but it might be wise to practice "social distancing."

STAY INFORMED

Being close to your pastor means being another set of eyes and ears. One of the abilities I have developed over time is to stay informed.

I read, I listen, I watch for trends and information, even outside the confines of my church, that could improve or affect our ministry. The more I learn, the more plans I can implement to make our ministry more effective. We are all part of the same body, regardless of which local church we belong to, and we can learn from each other to grow stronger and be better ministers for the Lord. The more informed we are, the better growth strategies we can develop and the quicker we can provide one another feedback and advice on how to handle certain situations that arise.

HANDLING INFORMATION

Your proximity to your pastor will sometimes expose you to issues and situations that are sensitive and private. If you are the kind of person who always has to talk, your ability to develop trust will quickly diminish. You have to understand the weight of the responsibility of being close to a pastor. Tact and faithfulness are key ingredients to developing a successful relationship. I do not even share the delicate matters I am privy to with my wife. She knows nothing of what I discuss with my pastor. You have to learn to be a depository of information and a releaser of none. Church is a place where trust is expected and required because people need to be able to share their struggles. Should you be privy to such information, keeping your mouth shut is necessary to build and maintain trust. You cannot be everyone's friend and share everything you know with everyone all over town. People who are always talking among others have a hard time keeping information private, but absolute discretion and respect for privacy is required for this role.

Imagine your pastor pouring his or heart out to you or someone else where you happen to be present. Imagine the level of trust it takes for your pastor to speak freely while expecting trust from those present. How can you then share your pastor's story with others? I find it unthinkable, but it is pertinent to talk about this so you understand how much wisdom and tact it takes to be in a position of trust and closeness to your pastor. You must possess the unequivocal confidence of your pastor if you are going to be a successful ladder holder.

UNDERSTAND THE
RELATIONSHIP

"Faithless is he that says farewell when the road darkens."
— J. R. R. Tolkien —

I t is easy to appear to be an expert at parenting until you become
a parent. It is easy to appear to be a relationship expert until you
experience the challenges of building one. It is also easy to criticize
leadership and take it for granted until you become a leader. Suddenly
you realize things are not what you thought they were. When you have
not walked in someone else's shoes, it is very easy to judge that person
by his or her actions while you judge yourself by your motives.

Hands down, pastoring has to be one of the most difficult jobs in
life. Many times, I have wondered why anyone would desire to be a
pastor unless he or she was called into it. Pastors are among the most
misunderstood and taken for granted. The good news, however, is that
when God calls someone into ministry, He also calls others to support
that individual at various points along his or her journey.

A perfect example that shows what pastors deal with can be found
in Numbers 11 where the Israelites complained bitterly about their lives
and all that God was doing for them. God had just delivered them from
the Egyptians, who treated them as slaves, beat them, and made life
unbearable. God appointed Moses to deliver them from the Egyptian

captivity and lead them to the Promised Land. Unfortunately, on their way there, they complained about everything during their time in the wilderness, even when God gave them manna to eat.

> "Oh, for some meat!" they exclaimed. "We remember the fish we used to eat for free in Egypt. And we had all the cucumbers, melons, leeks, onions, and garlic we wanted. But now our appetites are gone. All we ever see is this manna!" (Numbers 11:4b-6, NLT)

The scripture says their complaints came up to the ears of the Eternal One, who then sent fire to destroy His own people. Moses interceded on their behalf, however, and God stopped the destruction.

> Moses heard all the families standing in the doorways of their tents whining, and the Lord became extremely angry. Moses was also very aggravated. And Moses said to the Lord, "Why are you treating me, your servant, so harshly? Have mercy on me! What did I do to deserve the burden of all these people? Did I give birth to them? Did I bring them into the world? Why did you tell me to carry them in my arms like a mother carries a nursing baby? How can I carry them to the land you swore to give their ancestors? Where am I supposed to get meat for all these people? They keep whining to me, saying, 'Give us meat to eat!' I can't carry all these people by myself! The load is far too heavy! If this is how you intend to treat me, just go ahead and kill me. Do me a favor and spare me this misery!" (Numbers 11:10-15, NLT)

Look at what Moses was going through just pastoring the people he had been called to lead. He came to the point where he even asked

God to do him a favor and kill him! Many of us tout Moses as one of the great leaders in the Bible, and truly he was, but look at how much of a struggle it was for him to pastor the people God had called him to lead.

Pastoring is a tough job. Imagine being called to lead a people and to be a representative of God in their lives.. Imagine these same people refusing to go through the disciplines that nurture Christian maturity, always having to depend on you for the very things they ought to have mastered in order to help others. Imagine constantly counseling the very people you preach to weekly, giving them the wisdom keys to the issues they deal with. Imagine being on call 24/7 to lead a group of people, some of whom expect nothing less than total attention whenever they need it, with no regard for the pastor's personal needs or family. Imagine dealing with unnecessary squabbles from people who refuse to grow or apply the lifesaving word and principles that you teach from the pulpit every week.

I have seen people leave church and walk away from a pastor because they disagree with just one message he or she has preached. Imagine loving selflessly and being committed to a people who love only conditionally, and you never know whether they'll stand with you when you need them. Some of the times I have seen my pastor hurt the most is when people he had faithfully supported just walked out on him without ever giving a reason. I have seen people my pastor helped through some very tough times get back on their feet after many hours, days, months, and even years of counseling and financial help, and then suddenly not have time for church anymore.

> Imagine loving selflessly and being committed to a people who love only conditionally, and you never know whether they'll stand with you when you need them.

"Being a pastor is like death by a thousand paper cuts," says Rev. Dr. Ken Fong, senior pastor at Evergreen Baptist Church in Rosemead, California, and a program director at Fuller Theological Seminary in Pasadena. "You're scrutinized and criticized from top to bottom, stem to stern. You work for an invisible, perfect Boss, and you're supposed to lead a ragtag gaggle of volunteers toward God's coming future. It's like herding cats, but harder." I smiled when I read this from Dr. Fong, but he certainly knows the immense weight of being a pastor. Even *Forbes* categorized pastoring as one of the most challenging jobs. Let's see their rankings:

- #9: CEO
- #8: Congressman/Congresswoman
- #7: Newspaper editor
- #6: Mayor
- **#5: Pastor/minister**
- #4: Football coach
- #3: Second in command in any organization
- #2: University president
- #1: Stay-at-home-parent

You'll notice that *Forbes* ranks "Pastor/minister" as the fifth toughest job. Let's consider some of the statistics surrounding pastors in ministry now:

- Eighty percent believe pastoral ministry has negatively affected their families, and many pastors' kids do not attend church because of what it has done to their parents.
- A quarter of pastors' families resent the church and its effect on their families.
- Seventy-eight percent of pastors report having their vacation and personal time interrupted constantly with ministry duties and expectations.
- Seventy percent of pastors report that they do not have anyone they call a close friend.
- Fifty-four percent of pastors (that's more than one in every two) find the role of a pastor overwhelming.

- Forty-eight percent of pastors feel the demands of ministry are more than they can handle.
- More than 50 percent of pastors believe their hardest job is to recruit committed volunteers who will stand with them.
- Eighty percent of pastors expect conflict in their church.
- Seventy percent of pastors claim to have a lower self-esteem now than they did when they entered the ministry.
- According to a Gallup 2018 poll, Americans' trust in faith leaders and pastors fell to a record low of 37 percent, ranking below multiple medical professions, teachers, and police, and just above journalists.
- Eighty-four percent of pastors are lonely and desire to have a close relationship with someone they can trust and confide in.

These are a few of the harrowing statistics depicting the current trends of pastoring. Take a look at Hebrews 13:17-19:

> Obey your spiritual leaders and recognize their authority, for they keep watch over your soul without resting since they will have to give an account to God for their work. So it will benefit you when you make their work a pleasure and not a heavy burden. (Hebrews 13:17-19, TPT)

In this scripture, the word *resting* comes from the Greek word *agrypnein*, which is often used for staying awake through the night. This is literally what happens to pastors. I have seen my pastor come out of counseling meetings, appearing as though he just got out of a fight. Pastors carry the burdens and secrets of so many people that it can literally keep them up at night. The Message Translation for the Hebrews scripture says:

"Be responsive to your pastoral leaders. Listen to their counsel. They are alert to the condition of your lives and work under the strict supervision of God. Contribute to the joy of their leadership, not its drudgery. Why would you want to make things harder for them?" (Hebrews 13:17-19, MSG)

We are admonished to contribute to their joy and not to make things harder for them because of the weight of the responsibility God has placed on them. Many pastors are quietly screaming for God to send them their Joshuas because they are tired of carrying the weight all by themselves or possibly with a few others. The only way a pastor can accomplish what God called him or her to do is with faithful and loyal people behind him or her. Your pastor can never accomplish the vision alone. Even John the Baptist had disciples or people close to him at some point.

A day in the life of a pastor can be very daunting. One of our close ministry partners made a comment to my pastor recently, which is shown herein:

"I think maybe people need to understand the courage it takes to do what pastors do every day. I imagine you preaching a message on the topic 'Be a pastor for a week,' which lays out the typical challenges within just one week of pastoring. From the financial challenges, close people leaving and creating a gap that is hard to fill, parenting your own kids, new churches springing up nearby, resolving dramatic crises in people's lives, managing your reputation constantly as people broadcast lies, being a husband, the constant tension between growth and resting in what you've achieved, etc. the truth is that beneath all the preaching, you are running

a company with a volunteer force. Incredibly difficult to
do." (Ms. Pearl Nartey)

Ms. Pearl Nartey nailed the challenge so succinctly. A lot of pastors
have to constantly dabble in uncertainty by virtue of the work they've
been called to. They even put their own families on the line for the sake
of their ministry. They never know who is going to leave tomorrow or
whether their people will still keep supporting the vision. I have seen
this with my pastor, especially in the early stages of ministry where the
disparity between the vision and the people he had was the greatest.

It is clear that a pastor's job is difficult, which is why I am writing
this chapter to those who feel they've been called to hold their pastor's
hands in ministry. I call them *the Behind the Scenes* servants. These are
people God calls to be ladder holders or servants behind the scenes, who
are absolutely sold out to the well-being and vision of the pastor. They
are not in this role for any recognition, nor do they have any di-vision.
They are focused on the one vision they have been called to support, and
they remain on course regardless of the discomfort it may cause. They
are fiercely loyal, don't have many friends, and desire nothing but to
assist the visionary in seeing the realization of the vision. These people
are not interested in any public recognition and are content just to see
progress being made in achieving their pastor's vision.

THE RESPONSIBILITY

The term *ladder holder* has been used by many but especially Dr. Sam
Chand. According to him, ladder holders are people in support roles
to the pastor and whose input directly impacts the effectiveness of the
pastor and his or her vision. This is a loaded responsibility, knowing your
role directly impacts the pastor's ability to effectively deliver and stay on
course. This is not a role you should seek to occupy just to have access to
the pastor to meet your needs. Some people seek leadership or volunteer

roles just to impress upon others that they have access to the pastor. But that is not a valid reason for taking on the role of ladder holder.

The biggest responsibility you have is to build and maintain the trust, confidence, and well-being of your pastor. Pastors have a calling and vision given to them by God but have to depend on men, mostly volunteers, to bring it to pass. I have heard many say it is God's church and God will build His church Himself. I do not subscribe to that school of thought, however, because if that were so, no church would have issues, and every church would be filled to the brim with revived and hungry Christians. God builds His church through people like you and me, and every vision requires committed servants who bear the responsibility of supporting the vision to help make it happen. Let's not over-spiritualize the church. It takes a partnership between God and faithful people to build it, and it takes wisdom and skill to effectively grow it. There are basic requirements for building and growing any organization that have nothing to do with prayer or being spiritual. It is possible to be less spiritually inclined but build a better organization than someone who is deeply spiritual but lacks the know-how.

> God builds His church through people like you and me, and every vision requires committed servants who bear the responsibility of supporting the vision to help make it happen.

Being close to your pastor is not a role to take lightly. You cannot be on and off whenever you choose. You cannot be supportive today and pull back your service and support on a whim. You have to buy into the vision of the pastor you have been called to support, and you must know that vision inside out. It must resonate within you until it becomes part of you. This is what will keep you loyal to your pastor and committed to the vision. I have been loyal to my pastor from the first day our paths crossed. I have accepted his vision of restoring the broken and have learned over time how to make it my own. You cannot adequately provide this sort of dependable support if you have not come to the place of total conviction.

There are many examples of such relationships in the Bible and in real life today that we can point to. Consider how the relationship between Moses and Joshua developed over time. Moses spent his time pouring himself into and mentoring Joshua while Joshua studiously served and understudied Moses. There is also David and Jonathan, Elijah and Elisha, Paul and Timothy, and many more. In all these relationships, you see a deep commitment to an individual and what they stand for and the consistency of that commitment. You cannot claim to be committed to a person or a vision and not be consistent in both presence and attention.

Another key responsibility is your ability to anticipate the needs of your pastor and ensure that you act on them. You must know and understand what is required of you when you are in a close support role to your pastor. I have moments when I just sit and think about the week, month, or quarter ahead, drawing various scenarios in my mind and on paper, trying to anticipate the various needs of my pastor and what it will take to meet those needs. On numerous occasions my pastor has asked me to do a particular thing and I would tell him it is already done or in progress. Such responses let him know he has ladder holders he can trust. This relationship was not built overnight, but over a long period of time where I had to demonstrate my capacity for the role I occupy.

Every level of responsibility requires you to demonstrate your ability to effectively occupy the role and an innate potential for growth and accomplishment. Remember that your attitude, commitment, and work ethic at any level will always determine whether you end up being promoted to the next level. It was during my time as a music director that I demonstrated my ability

> You cannot claim to be committed to a vision or someone and not exhibit the consistency in presence and attention it requires.

to advance into a closer support role as a ladder holder. In that capacity, there are four key parts of me I consider essential to effectively discharge my role:

- My hands
- My ears
- My eyes
- My mouth

My hands are essential to hold the ladder, keep it steady, and to *physically* support the vision. My hands are also indicative of my skill. I just can't hold a ladder by pressing my thumb against the frame. The ladder will only stand upright if my hands are holding it in a firm and decisive way. So be careful when you assume you are doing your part in building your church or organization by simply touching the ladder with your occasional presence.

My ears allow me to listen to the instructions of my pastor. They are tuned to his voice to ensure I hear every communication necessary for me to discharge my duties or to adjust my grip or strategy on the ground.

The eyes allow me to do two things: 1) to observe my pastor to ensure I see communication that is not vocalized, and 2) to be watchful of my surroundings, as they have a direct impact on my ability to keep holding the ladder effectively. Being aware of your surroundings helps you provide useful feedback to the visionary so he or she may adjust or respond accordingly as needed.

My mouth gives me the ability to verify the instructions I receive from my pastor and to provide feedback. It helps me to communicate with those around me and the visionary on the ladder.

Your ability to take care of something that belongs to another man or woman is directly related to how others will support you in due season. So hold the ladder like your life depends on it. Do it like you would for a dignitary you have the utmost respect for. If your leader has to constantly look behind him or her, not knowing whether someone will hold the ladder, then he or she can never make adequate progress.

THE ONESIPHOROUS EXAMPLE

One of the most significant but least talked-about people in the Bible is a gentleman called Onesiphorous. His story is highlighted in 2 Timothy 1:16. Onesiphorous was supposedly one of the seventy disciples chosen and sent by Jesus to preach. The text is brief but loaded with revelation on how he related with Paul. His faithfulness is highlighted in the following scripture:

> Nevertheless, so many times Onesiphorus was like a breath of fresh air to me and never seemed to be ashamed of my chains. May our Lord Jesus bestow compassion and mercy upon him and his household. For when he arrived in Rome, he searched and searched for me until he found out where I was being held, so that he could minister to me, just like he did so wonderfully as I rested in his house while in Ephesus, as you well know. (2 Timothy 1:16-18, TPT)

When Paul wrote this letter to Timothy, he was in prison in Rome, during a time of great persecution of Christians. This was during the reign of Nero, a young Roman Emperor born a generation after the death and resurrection of Christ. At some point during his reign, Nero went out on a limb to have Christians killed as a way to deflect responsibility after he was accused of setting the Great Fire that decimated most of Rome. Because most of his people believed his claim that the Christians were the ones who set the fire, this generated the passion and drive to get Christians killed as a way to placate the anger of the Romans. This is what made Rome a dangerous city for Christians.

Then comes Onesiphorous, who Paul described as a breath of fresh air to him. The scripture says he disregarded the dangers to his own life when he was in Rome and "searched and searched" until he found where Paul was being held so he could minister to him. His commitment to refresh Paul was so great that he refused to let the dangers of being caught or persecuted prevent him from seeking to be a blessing to Paul. He knew seeking out Paul could cost him his own life, but he persisted in his unwavering desire to see his pastor refreshed. The testimony of Paul regarding Onesiphorous is one that all servants ought to desire in their service. His commitment to Paul was based on conviction and not convenience.

Onesiphorous was considered great in Paul's eyes for another reason: his gratitude. He was part of those who gave their lives to Christ through Paul's ministry at Ephesus. Onesiphorous had visited Paul in Ephesus before Paul was taken prisoner. He was grateful for Paul's sacrifice as he encountered many dangers just to bring the gospel to them. From the time of his conversion, Onesiphorous became part of the church that Paul started in Ephesus and always determined to be a blessing to him. He considered what Paul had done for him as priceless and made it his aim to refresh Paul whenever possible. So when he heard that Paul was in prison in Rome after the Great Fire, he set off on this dangerous journey to search for and refresh him. He made it his ministry.

Every pastor needs an Onesiphorous in their life and ministry because he or she is always on an arduous journey, one that wears him or her out almost constantly. This is why they need people who commit to be there for them and support their call.

This is also the reason why more true and loyal servants are needed in the body, servants who are committed to the end and count it an honor to be in such a position. If you desire to be the kind of servant who seeks to always refresh your pastor, you cannot effectively do it outside of a strong, unwavering conviction, which is unassailable by the whims and whisperings of men. You need the kind of commitment that is not affected even by people walking away and leaving your pastor's ministry, often for trivial reasons.

The conviction for your commitment must also never be one that is affected by the changing seasons of ministry. Not every day in ministry is a rosy walk in the park. There were days I did not even want to see our church building or serve the body again, but the conviction and commitment to serve kept me at the helm of my service boat, dedicated to the cause. I understood that I was responsible for my commitment to support my pastor, and it was not something I could pray to receive. It was a behavior I had to cultivate. I do not believe in praying for commitment. It is a teachable behavior we are all capable of cultivating. It is a decision. Committing to serve in your church and honor your pastor with your loyalty means not allowing yourself to compromise on that decision. You cannot commit to serve in a role or support your pastor and be the first to walk out at the slightest offense or discomfort. You have to be immune to offense and seek nothing but to be present to support the vision.

> If you desire to be the kind of servant that seeks to always refresh your pastor, you cannot effectively do it outside of a strong, unwavering conviction, which is unassailable by the whims and whisperings of men.

SEEK WISDOM

Over the years, I have grown from being a music director to be the operations director, responsible for ensuring we have the right systems in place for achieving our vision. This role places me in my pastor's presence constantly as we deliberate on vision, strategy, and church issues. My number-one need in such a role is wisdom. Wisdom, in the context of this topic, is the quality of having experience, knowledge, and good judgment. Having this quality is essential to knowing what to say, when to say it, and most importantly, what not to say while engaged in your role.

James 1:5 says, "...if any of you lacks wisdom, let him ask of God, who gives to all liberally and without reproach, and it will be given to him." The literal translation of this scripture is something like "...since you lack wisdom, ask of me..." This is a promise to us that God will give us wisdom if we ask.

I have always been careful how and when I approach my pastor. I have grown to be able to interpret his facial expression and feel his state of mind. Because I have my pastor's ear, it is important I don't contaminate his spirit by saying anything inappropriate or wrongly timed.

It is also very important that I give my pastor wise counsel so he is not blindsided by any issues. I have prayed for wisdom and spiritual revelation daily by quoting the following scripture:

> "...that the God of our Lord Jesus Christ, the Father of glory, may give to you the spirit of wisdom and revelation in the knowledge of Him, the eyes of your understanding being enlightened; that you may know what is the hope of His calling, what are the riches of the glory of His inheritance in the saints, and what is the exceeding greatness of His power toward us who believe, according to the working of His mighty power." (Ephesians 1:17-19 NKJV)

I memorized this scripture soon after I started serving under my pastor and make sure I recite it every day. I set a daily reminder on my phone for 9 a.m. so I can pray this prayer consistently. I can certainly testify that I have seen it work in my life so tremendously over the years.

SHARE THE BURDEN

Many years ago, I sought the Lord to put me in a place in my pastor's life where I could share his burden. I saw the emotional burden he carried because of the weight of the calling on his life, and I wanted to help. I just didn't know how. One day, I asked God to place some of my pastor's burdens on me anytime things got tough and he needed help. It was just a simple prayer, but I wanted to share his burden in those moments. In case you are oblivious to this fact, pastors go through their own challenges and fight the same battles we do; they actually fight bigger battles by virtue of the role they occupy. Their calling does not exempt them from personal challenges. I only asked God to help me share my pastor's ministry burden so his load could be a bit lighter.

I was not even aware there was a scripture in Numbers 11 that gives an account of Moses being so overburdened by the cares and complaints of his people that he asked God to kill him. So, God asked Moses to choose seventy men he knew to be leaders among the people so He could take some of His Spirit on Moses and place it on them so they could help ease the burdens of the people so Moses wouldn't have to carry them alone.

> Then the Lord said to Moses, "Gather before me seventy men who are recognized as elders and leaders of Israel. Bring them to the Tabernacle to stand there with you. I will come down and talk to you there. I will take some of the Spirit that is upon you, and I will put the Spirit upon them also. They will bear the burden of the people along with you, so you will not have to carry it alone. (Numbers 11:16-17, NLT)

When I first read this scripture, I saw it as God placing an anointing on some men to help Moses lead the people. I lost the whole point about the people being selected to use the anointing they had been given to share the burden and weight of the people.

When I prayed an earnest prayer for God to help me share the burden on my pastor, what happened was quite remarkable. There are times I would wake up or be in the middle of my workday and I would suddenly feel an emotional weight on me, just an odd feeling that had no bearing on how my day was progressing. It used to confuse me until I started praying about it. As I prayed, I would keep remembering the request I made of God years earlier to help me share my pastor's burden. I know the scripture in Numbers 11 also shows the people Moses selected taking over some of the responsibility of leading the people so Moses' load will be lighter. But over and above this is the spiritual burden that you can help your pastor bear spiritually what can be felt physically.

Up until this moment, I have never shared this, but I hope it will bless you to commit to stand in loyalty and pray to share the burden of your pastor, not just physically, but spiritually. Ask God to take a small part of the burden on your pastor and place it on you, so he or she does not feel overwhelmed.

DON'T MANIPULATE YOUR PASTOR OR HINDER THE VISION

I have seen some disturbing things in churches, but nothing infuriates me more than those who try to manipulate the pastor with their gift or contribution to the ministry. In a recent meeting where I had the chance to speak to some senior pastors, I boldly told them never to allow any person to use their gifts or resources to hold the ministry ransom. It is good and important to serve your way to a place of importance to the ministry and to your pastor, but never use that position to control others in your church just because you see yourself as important. And never have an overinflated opinion of yourself just because of what you contribute to your local church.

We have nothing that God did not give us. Every opportunity to serve as a volunteer or in a place of direct support to your pastor is a privilege. This means you were given a certain level of access, not because you deserve it, but because someone granted it out of his or her own free will. It is, therefore, unwise to use it to steer the church your way, by virtue of your position. No position you occupy in church must ever become your personal domain where everyone must bow to your rules or sit out.

Once when I was invited to attend a church's music program in North London, I arrived early, and as I sat at the back of building, waiting for the program to start, I saw a gentleman who appeared to be a leader giving multiple instructions to other volunteers at the front of the church. They did not own the building they used for church, so they had to set up and tear down after every service. As I watched them set up, I realized this individual was abusing the volunteers who had come to help him set up. He was being rude and yelling at them as they scurried to complete the setup. I was shocked at the language he was using and the attitude he was showing, on full display for all to see. He did not even seem to care that visitors had started arriving. He was intent on demonstrating what he thought was leadership—exerting control over the people he leads.

When the program was over, I asked the gentleman who invited me who that man was and why he was so rude. He told me the gentleman was a leader who felt nothing in the church could work without his input. He had grown so seemingly entrenched in his role that he thought he could treat people any way he wanted. He felt he was doing the pastor a favor by being so diligent to complete his tasks, and that's all that mattered. Apparently, his attitude was a known issue both to leadership and to the church members.

This gentleman was apparently useful to the church and the pastor or he wouldn't have been trusted with leadership. He was dependable, available, and made things happen, probably without supervision or instruction. But it appears this had gone to his head and he felt he could behave however he wanted without repercussions. He probably felt no one could rebuke him, not even the pastor. Apparently, he was right. I found out this had been going on for years, and he had never been corrected. I also learned that some of the members had left the church because they could not tolerate this man's attitude, nor understand why the church's leadership had been allowing this to go on for such a long time.

This is a clear case of manipulation where one individual over-estimated his importance to the ministry and thought the church leadership couldn't touch him because of his contribution. From all accounts, he was available, knowledgeable, and committed to the church. But as much as these are desirable qualities for a servant to possess, the attitude these qualities come wrapped in is probably even more important. This gentleman may be able to do a lot in terms of building the church, but if none of the members can work with him because of the way he treats them, then what's the point? While the church was trying to gather members, he was busy scattering them with his attitude because he thought his gift was more important than the souls of the men and women the church was trying to gather. I am not sure what happened to that church, but I am certain achieving their vision would not be a smooth-sailing experience as long as they had this bottleneck among them.

Be careful when you begin to feel your contribution to a ministry is so important that the thought of being indispensable begins to come to your mind. Be very careful when you begin to think your gift is yours and you can leave anytime you don't agree with the way the leadership is running the church. Be careful when you think your gift and contribution is what carries the ministry. Be careful when you think that all decisions must come through you, and that you will not contribute to anything done outside your purview. It is a prideful spirit intent on hindering the vision.

One associate pastor in a church I once served in as music director got upset with me because I questioned his attitude and rudeness in how he spoke to most of us. In response, he told me I never to go on his stage with "my choir." He said I had no right to question the way a pastor speaks or behaves. To punish me for this apparent audacity, he told me not to stand on the stage at any time during the church service. He used to come early to set up a platform to use during the service, but he told me it was for the pastor to preach from and not for me and the choir. He instructed us to stand on the floor and not on the platform anytime we had to minister.

Here was a man who was prepared to compromise our corporate worship because he was upset with me for questioning his attitude to many people. He obviously had an overinflated opinion of his importance to the ministry. Of course, he was the go-to person for all things church—a totally dependable and committed person. But is that enough to warrant such behavior from him? I don't think so. He was in a position where he could help the senior pastor achieve the vision of the house of God, but instead he chose to hinder it with his behavior. Many people refused to serve just because they didn't want to deal with him. This cannot be a good testimony to have—that people refuse to serve because of you. It is an indictment against what the church stands for. Like the human body, each part is important, and each plays a different role. So don't laud your apparent importance over others or silently threaten to withhold your contribution if anyone offends you. You'd be fighting the very One who gave you the gift and opportunity to use it. That's certainly not wise.

FAMILIARITY—YOUR BIGGEST ENEMY

Let me start off by saying that your pastor is not your friend to banter with. Your pastor is not one you forward indecent jokes to on social media. If you happen to know where your pastor lives, it is not a privilege to abuse by choosing to appear at his or her home anytime you choose, just to hang out. Even if your pastor thinks it is okay to do any of the above, please do not do it. As much as it lies with you, consciously keep a distance between you and your pastor. Your pastor is your spiritual leader who provides oversight over your soul, without resting. It is your responsibility to put in all checks and balances to ensure the wall of reverence is never broken. Having walked closely with my pastor for over twenty-five years, it has been absolutely pertinent for me to do whatever it takes to stay away from familiarity, which does more to erode the effectiveness of a relationship than any other known vice.

Familiarity means to know someone or something so well that it causes you to lose your admiration, respect, and sense of awe. It means taking the relationship for granted by being a little too casual with the person or thing you used to hold sacred and dignified. Even though it is not always a deliberate intention to become too familiar with someone, every relationship will flow into the realm of the familiar if conscious effort is not made to maintain a sense of awe. It happens in marriages, parenting, friendships, churches, places of employment...the list goes on. It is a constant in life. Maintaining your sense of awe and respect for a relationship or a thing takes deliberate effort.

A congregation can also become so unconsciously familiar with the gift of their pastor that his or her service to them becomes commonplace. Many times you will see a pastor show so much more power and a keen demonstration of gifts when he or she is in an environment that's different from the usual crowd of followers. Jesus Himself experienced familiarity to the extent that He, the miracle worker, could not work miracles in His own backyard.

> Afterward, Jesus left Capernaum and returned with his disciples to Nazareth, his hometown. On the Sabbath, he went to teach in the synagogue. Everyone who heard his teaching was overwhelmed with astonishment. They said among themselves, "What incredible wisdom has been

given to him! Where did he receive such profound insights? And what mighty miracles flow through his hands! Isn't this Mary's son, the carpenter, the brother of Jacob, Joseph, Judah, and Simon? And don't his sisters all live here in Nazareth?" And they took offense at him. Jesus said to them, "A prophet is treated with honor everywhere except in his own hometown, among his relatives, and in his own house." He was unable to do any great miracle in Nazareth, except to heal a few sick people by laying his hands upon them. He was amazed at the depth of their unbelief! Then Jesus went out into the different villages and taught the people. (Mark 6:1-6, TPT)

This account used to baffle me. I used to wonder why Jesus couldn't overrule the familiarity of His own kindred and work miracles among them as would be expected of someone like Him. Then one day it struck me that familiarity can be so powerful that it can limit even God from working through His servants. While Jesus was busy teaching and edifying them, they chose instead to make His humanness so big that they missed the visitation. They got so familiar with each other that in their eyes nothing great could come out of their town. Such was the power of this mental block that even Jesus could not override it. The force of familiarity has stunted the growth of more churches than many other known sins. It can reduce the voice of the one whom God has elected to speak into your life to nothing. How can you make progress if you do not esteem the voice of God when He speaks through your pastor?

> Even though it is not always a deliberate intention to become too familiar with someone, every relationship will flow into the realm of the familiar if conscious effort is not made to maintain a sense of awe.

I value the words of my pastor more than any other person I know. When he sends a text or simply says "Thank you, God bless you," I take it very seriously. Recently he sent a text that said, "May

God remember your household." That very morning, I asked God to honor the words of His servant. I said, "If my pastor is the one God has appointed in my life as my spiritual authority, then those words cannot fail." I demanded the manifestation of those words from God. I believed without a shadow of doubt that God would honor that word.

When it's time for the benediction at church, I get excited. That is when my pastor pronounces prayer, blessings, and well wishes over the church before we disperse. Of course, I make sure I take in every word pronounced over us just so I have something to hold on to and expect in my life. There have been many times my pastor has casually spoken a word over me in passing and it has happened just because I honored the word as God's words spoken through His servant to me. If this is my understanding, how can I take him for granted and become his friend? I can find many other friends, but I can't find another man of God whom He specifically chose to watch over me. I've been serving under my pastor for twenty-five years, and I still get the jitters when I see his name on my phone, calling me. I usually do a super quick inventory of my day's actions to see if I have done something wrong. I know it sounds funny but it's just an unconscious reaction. I still bow when I shake his hand when greeting him because I respect what I honor. It is not prudent to try to demonstrate to others that you know your pastor personally. I do not even approve putting pictures of me and my pastor on my social media page. Not that there is something particularly wrong with it, but I choose not to do it.

In December 2019, I accompanied my pastor to the City of Toronto for a program, and, after one of the services, I saw people line up to take pictures with him. At that point I remembered I had only two pictures of the two of us in our twenty-five years of knowing each other. The first was taken when he formally introduced me to the church in London in 1995, and the second was taken at a conference we both spoke at in London in 2016. So I asked him if I could take another picture with him. It wasn't because I couldn't have asked him for one in the past, but because the deep reverence I have deliberately cultivated over the years prevented me from seemingly normal requests.

CORPORATE FAMILIARITY

Sometimes a church or group can develop such a familiarity with a vision that a negative status quo also develops that prevents others who are willing to support the vision from making an impact. There are a number of accounts of this in the Bible. Jesus made a remarkable statement to this effect in Luke 7:44:

> Then turning toward the woman, He said to Simon, "Do you see this woman? I came into your house [but you failed to extend to Me the usual courtesies shown to a guest]; you gave Me no water for My feet, but she has wet My feet with her tears and wiped them with her hair [demonstrating her love]. You gave Me no [welcoming] kiss, but from the moment I came in, she has not ceased to kiss My feet. You did not [even] anoint My head with [ordinary] oil, but she has anointed My feet with [costly and rare] perfume. (Luke 7:44-46, AMP)

This is part of the account of a Pharisee who invited Jesus to his home for dinner. In those days, people did not travel just for leisure the way we do now. They traveled only when they had to, in hot, dusty, treacherous environments, and usually on foot. So upon entering someone's home, the host would greet his guests with a kiss on each cheek and offer water for their tired, dirty feet. If available, he would also offer some perfumed ointment to soothe and freshen them up. But the Pharisee did not do that for Jesus when He entered his home. He took Jesus for granted and never even extended Him the expected courtesies of the time. But in comes this lady, the star of the story:

> And behold, a woman in the city who was a sinner, when she knew that Jesus sat at the table in the Pharisee's house, brought an alabaster flask of fragrant oil, and stood at His feet behind Him weeping; and she began to wash His feet with her tears, and wiped them with the hair of her head; and she kissed His feet and anointed them with the fragrant oil. Now when the Pharisee who had invited Him saw this, he spoke to himself, saying, "This Man, if He were a prophet, would know who and what manner of woman this is who is touching Him, for she is a sinner." (Luke 7:37-39, NKJV)

She walked in, broke protocol, and walked straight to Jesus and worshipped. She came prepared with her alabaster flask of fragrant oil and broke it to wash His feet. She was certainly deliberate in her intentions to worship. While men stood beside this interesting spectacle and questioned her act, she was busy serving and providing the reverence the host failed to provide.

This is similar to what sometimes happens in our churches and in our relationships. You walk into a church and love it so much that you commit to serve, but somehow the guardians of the status quo prevent you from helping to support the vision the way you want to. People tend to look at you weird if you join the church and yet refuse to join their cliques. The status quo defines what is normal acceptable behavior within the church, and frown on anyone who tries to operate outside their standards. This is what I call "corporate familiarity." A church or a group can be so familiar or rigid in their way of doing things that it prevents others from expressing their worship through service. A group of choristers can get so familiar with each other that they frown on anyone who comes in with the right skillset to help move the choir to another level. They question the leader with murmurings and attitude when he allows a newer member the opportunity to lead a song when older members have been waiting or desiring to do so. Never mind the fact that they are obviously not as skilled as the newer member.

One sure sign of familiarity is when someone begins to despise or question another simply for doing what was expected of him or her in the first place. The people stood by Jesus without observing the proper protocols, but when someone broke through the wall and worshipped, they had a problem with it. She had a revelation of who Jesus is and did not hold back in showing reverence and giving true worship. When the establishment gets familiar with the vision, the gatekeepers will always prevent and restrain the very people who come in to help and make a change. Do not let this ever prevent you from serving. If you feel inclined or called to serve your church and support your pastor, do not let anyone change your mind or pollute your desire. Break through the barriers and stay committed.

THE IMPORTANCE OF COVERING

I cannot complete this chapter without talking about the importance of being under the right spiritual covering and connecting to the one who covers you. Some have erroneously believed this is not necessary as long as you can read your Bible and pray on your own because God is everyone's Father. Indeed, God is our Father, but He has given some to be shepherds over us in this life.

Throughout the Epistles attributed to the Apostle Paul, we read of him addressing the church as his children he had begotten. He presented himself as a father who had labored for them and who continued to admonish and encourage them to keep following the instructions he gave them. Let's look at an example in 1 Corinthians 4:15:

> "For though you may have ten thousand teachers in Christ, you do not have many fathers."

Paul spiritually fathered the Corinthian church when he preached and presented the good news, which got them converted. He provided guidance and corrected them when they were wrong. He prayed for them and cheered for them as a true father would do. He even chastised them if the occasion called for it.

I learned a lot from the experience of journeying through fatherhood. I came to understand a lot about covering. I came to understand how my life example spoke louder to my children than my words did. I came to understand how my spiritual connection to them made it my responsibility to protect them regardless of how good or bad they are. I also came to understand how the guidance I provided them was critical to their development. I stand in a place where I know it is my responsibility to protect them physically and spiritually. I also know how important my prayers are to their progress in life because of my spiritual connection to them. I understand how my intercession for my children can protect them from imminent danger and potential repercussions from bad choices. This is what covering is. In the same way, your pastor provides a spiritual covering over you. Yes, I know that as children of God we have the Holy Spirit, but the same God put us in a local church and appoints a pastor to provide leadership and spiritual covering through Him. Hebrews 13:17 tells us to:

> "Obey those who rule over you, and be submissive, for
> they watch out for your souls, as those who must give
> an account."

Why would the writer of Hebrews admonish us to be submissive to our leaders as they watch over our souls? It is because God has appointed them to watch over us and provide a covering while we walk in this life. This is the covering your pastor provides. It is also the responsibility for which every pastor must give an account.

Let us look at the example of Moses when he led the children of Israel into the wilderness and they upset God by building a golden calf to worship. This is one of the most poignant examples of how a man can negotiate with God on behalf of another. It is quite a surreal encounter. In Exodus 24, we see God calling Moses to come up Mount Sinai so He may give him His commandments for His people. This encounter took forty days and forty nights, which was a long time in the eyes of the people. Eventually they came to the conclusion that they could not wait for Moses any longer and decided to use the jewelry they had plundered from the Egyptians to make a golden calf and recognize this idol as their god, the One who brought them out of Egypt. How intelligent!

This stirred up God's anger tremendously against the Israelites so much that He wanted to destroy them. The subsequent exchange between God and Moses is simply beautiful.:

> Then Moses pleaded with the Lord his God, and said: "Lord, why does Your wrath burn hot against Your people whom You have brought out of the land of Egypt with great power and with a mighty hand? Why should the Egyptians speak, and say, 'He brought them out to harm them, to kill them in the mountains, and to consume them from the face of the earth'? Turn from Your fierce wrath and relent from this harm to Your people. Remember Abraham, Isaac, and Israel, Your servants, to whom You swore by Your own self, and said to them, 'I will multiply your descendants as the stars of heaven; and all this land that I have spoken of I give to your descendants, and they shall inherit it forever.'" So the Lord relented from the harm which He said He would do to His people. (Exodus 32:11-14 NKJK)

Moses stood in the gap and provided a covering that God respected. So even when God Himself wanted to destroy His people, He was moved to relent after Moses pleaded with Him to be merciful toward His stiff-necked children. Moses "reminded" God of His promises to the patriarchs of Israel and why He had rescued them. This is a perfect example of covering.

Your pastor's covering is an intercessory position that has authority in the spiritual realm over your life and destiny. Your pastor's prayer and intercession for you has the ability to move you in the right direction and also to prevent certain situations from manifesting in your life. This is why you have to be connected to your pastor both physically and spiritually. In my life of service under my pastor, I have personally seen the rewards and benefits of submitting myself to him and recognizing the spiritual covering and authority he has over my life. I have been in situations where I've had to go to him for counsel, which in turn ended up saving me from trouble. In fact I went to him after receiving an unfavorable diagnosis from my doctor and received prayer, which strengthened me for what lay ahead. This is the importance of connecting to your pastor and respecting the covering he or she has over your life.

LOYALTY

"It's not about who is real in your face…it's about who stays loyal behind your back."

— Anon —

L oyalty is the willful choice to remain committed to those God has brought into our lives and has called us to serve, even when it costs us dearly. If there is one quality that is waning in the body of Christ today, I dare say it is loyalty. The appearance of so many options and the lack of a good foundation and understanding on the principles of loyalty have left many pastors and visions struggling for success. No vision can make any progress without the loyalty and support of the people who are called to move it forward. In like manner, no pastor can make significant progress without the loyalty of those called to support him or her.

The first foundation statement I'll make regarding loyalty is this:

> Loyalty is a decision you make in support of an endeavor or relationship, not an emotion you build up over time based on how a relationship or cause pans out in your evaluation.

Loyalty is a willing decision you make to support an endeavor, follow a cause, support a leader, or begin a covenant relationship. You cannot hold back loyalty from a cause or an individual you claim to support. It does not work. True loyalty closes out and removes other options you may have in relation to the cause you intend to support.

GOD AND US

Nothing gives a better depiction of true loyalty than God's stance toward us, His children. As frail and as inconsistent as we are, He still chooses to hitch Himself to us. He definitely knows what it means to be unequally yoked when it comes to loving us unconditionally and being committed to our wellbeing irrespective of our willingness to reciprocate commitment to Him. He put Himself in a profound place where He committed to love us whether we return that love to Him or not. He's totally steadfast in His unwavering love toward us regardless of our stance, and, because of that, He is duty bound to remain faithful to us. His loyalty to us is not dependent on any other circumstance or action; it is dependent solely on His nature and decision. 2 Timothy 2:13 NKJV says, "If we are faithless, He remains faithful; He cannot deny Himself." Consider the Message translation of Romans 8:37:

> None of this fazes us because Jesus loves us. I'm absolutely convinced that nothing—nothing living or dead, angelic or demonic, today or tomorrow, high or low, thinkable or unthinkable—absolutely nothing can get between us and God's love because of the way that Jesus our Master has embraced us. (Romans 8:37-38, MSG)

Absolutely nothing can come between us and God's love because of the way Jesus has embraced us! God's loyalty to us defies imagination and comprehension. It is rooted in the covenant He Himself established with us, sealed in the blood of His Son. It makes no sense that God would choose to be so loyal to such disloyal children, whom He has chosen to call His own. That my friends, is grace.

As a father, I look at my children and feel this unwavering love and loyalty to them that is independent of what they do or not do. It's an unconditional love and loyalty based simply on who they are to me and never on what they do. If I, being such an inconsistent human, can feel this toward my children, then how much more will God feel toward me and be dedicated to me simply because of who He is?

> God's loyal love couldn't have run out, His merciful love couldn't have dried up. They're created new every morning. How great your faithfulness! I'm sticking with God (I say it over and over). He's all I've got left. (Lamentations 3:22-24, MSG)

Who wouldn't want to know a God like this? Such a rich promise of loyalty even to those yet unborn.

I never had the chance to serve in the army, but there aren't many places you can see loyalty being displayed to the point of death. Being a frequent traveler, I tend to encounter many servicewomen and servicemen traveling to and from their bases at the airports. Cleon Raynor, Army Test and Evaluation Command (ATEC) operations division chief and a retired Army lieutenant colonel, once said so succinctly that:

> "Loyalty means commitment to a cause, a purpose, or a person. It embodies the ability to stand behind one's promises and convictions. Loyalty does not waiver in the time of test but garners strength from within to stand committed to support the person, the belief, or the cause despite whatever challenges may come."

According to Colonel Raynor, loyalty embodies the ability to stand behind one's promises and convictions. This means you don't get cold feet or let circumstances dictate your behavior when the conditions under which you pledged your loyalty changes. Loyalty requires a strong, unyielding commitment to support a person or the cause for which he or she stands. Character is the bedrock of loyalty, and, as someone mentioned to me recently, there is a flaw in your character if circumstances and opportunity control your loyalty. If your loyalty fades in the face of a trial or an unfavorable situation, then something is very wrong with your loyalty.

> There is a flaw in your character if circumstances and opportunity control your loyalty.

Loyalty also does not wane when the person you are loyal to is not around. Neither does it wane when you feel wronged or offended by the other party. In many churches, I see a lot of conditional loyalty because members attach their loyalty to the presence of the senior pastor. More often than not, in these churches, commitment, attendance, and giving drops when the senior pastor is away. They forget that loyalty is to a person and to that which he or she represents.

ELIJAH AND ELISHA

I find the story of Elijah and Elisha fascinating for various reasons. In 1 Kings 19:19-21, Elijah had just come off a great conquest at Mount Carmel where he had defeated Ahab's prophets by calling fire down from God to consume a sacrifice, and Ahab's prophets were not able to accomplish the same from their god, Baal. Also, Elijah killed all of King Ahab's the false prophets. As a result of this defeat, Jezebel, King Ahab's wife, swore to destroy Elijah, and he became afraid and ran off into the wilderness. During a subsequent discourse with God, God instructed him to go find Elisha and anoint him as prophet in his place.

> "So Elijah left that place and found Elisha son of Shaphat plowing a field with a team of oxen. He owned

twelve teams of oxen and was plowing with the twelfth team. Elijah came up to Elisha, took off his coat, and put it on Elisha. Then Elisha left his oxen and ran to follow Elijah. "Let me kiss my father and my mother goodbye," Elisha said. "Then I will go with you." Elijah answered, "Go back. It does not matter to me." So Elisha went back and took his pair of oxen and killed them. He used their wooden yoke for a fire. Then he cooked the meat and gave it to the people. After they ate it, Elisha left and followed Elijah and became his helper." (1 Kings 19:19-21, NCV)

In this scripture, we see Elijah finds Elisha plowing with twelve yoke of oxen, which means he came from a wealthy family and his future was probably secure, but God disrupted his life and sent Elijah to anoint him as his successor. I am sure Elisha was a man quietly searching for purpose in his heart prior to his encounter with Elijah. God has a way of locating and calling those who have searched for greater purpose in Him. If you are constantly wanting more out of Christian life, and you have a hunger and desire for some higher calling, keep believing, for God has a way of locating you.

After Elijah found Elisha, he killed the oxen; cooked the meat, using the wooden yoke as fuel for the fire; and gave it out to people. He basically sacrificed his inheritance and anything that could have caused him to return to his old life in case the walk got difficult. He gave it all up for the sake of the call. So, at this point, Elisha had no options outside of following his mentor, Elijah. Such was his desire to follow his master that he asked for a double portion of his anointing. In response, Elijah told Elisha that he would receive the double portion he asked for as he observed him being taken up.

And so it was, when they had crossed over, that Elijah said to Elisha, "Ask! What may I do for you, before I am taken away from you?" Elisha said, "Please let a double portion of your spirit be upon me." So he said, "You have asked a hard thing. Nevertheless, if you see me when I am taken from you, it shall be so for you; but if not, it shall not be so." Then it happened, as they continued on and talked, that suddenly a chariot of fire appeared with horses of fire and separated the two of them; and Elijah went up by a whirlwind into heaven. And Elisha saw it... (2 Kings 2:9-12 NKJV)

Elisha was given a condition that teaches us a lesson in loyalty. He had to be present and attentive in his service so he didn't miss the moment Elijah is taken away. True loyalty in a servant is signified by always being present to support. There are no off days. True loyalty will always result in action. It is not passively waiting for instruction before acting. Elisha's pursuit of purpose was so alive that he refused to get distracted or even rest when Elijah told him to wait behind. He understood God's call on his life and he was determined to stick with it until it was complete.

When I started working under my pastor in the City of London, I did not fully appreciate what I had signed up for. I didn't understand the full depth of what it would take to keep focused on the vision twenty-five years later. Remaining loyal to my pastor and the vision was not the problem; nothing could have prepared me enough for the work involved in building the church, or the battle I was about to fight when I began to lead people. But because of the foundation I had received when I started volunteering in church, I had no issues with loyalty. To an extent, I knew how to count the cost and take care of whatever was committed into my hands, but this thing called Life has a funny way of sometimes not letting things go the way you plan or expect to roll.

One day, I approached my pastor to complain about the choristers and the difficulties I was facing dealing with the people. He listened calmly and told me I have what it takes to handle it, so I should suit up and keep running! He said the last part in a stern voice, like a father correcting his son. He offered no words of support or sympathy. He basically told me to suck it up and get on with the job. That was more a rebuke from a father. If I was going to be successful in ministry, I had to learn how to deal with people while keeping my eyes on the vision and prize. People will always test your loyalty and your response to situations. Sometimes our bad choices and attitudes create situations in the very communities we serve in. This tests our loyalty to remain in the same place where we messed up.

What Colonel Raynor said in his quote means that inconsistency and instability can never be part of your fabric if you are to be trusted with supporting a vision. You cannot go to war with team members you do not trust to be there for you when the battle rages. You cannot be effective as a soldier when you constantly have to look behind you because you don't know whether everyone is in position. That can be exhausting and make you lose focus on the vision for which you stand.

Ruth pledged her loyalty to Naomi after her husband and father-in-law had passed. With grief in her heart, Ruth pledged to follow her mother-in-law to Judah, much against Naomi's initial wishes.

> Then they lifted up their voices and wept again; and Orpah kissed her mother-in-law, but Ruth clung to her. And she said, "Look, your sister-in-law has gone back to her people and to her gods; return after your sister-in-law." But Ruth said:
>
> "Entreat me not to leave you,
> Or to turn back from following after you;
> For wherever you go, I will go;
> And wherever you lodge, I will lodge;
> Your people shall be my people,
> And your God, my God.
> Where you die, I will die,

And there will I be buried.

The Lord do so to me, and more also,

If anything but death parts you and me."

(Ruth 1:14-17, NKJV)

This sad but beautiful story sees Ruth follow Naomi back to Bethlehem to begin life again. She served her mother-in-law faithfully, worked hard, and always followed her advice. This led Ruth to encounter Boaz, a rich relative of her late father-in-law, Elimelech. Boaz took a keen interest in Ruth, granted her favor, and eventually married her. She conceived and gave birth to a son named Obed. Obed fathered Jesse, who then fathered David.

> So Boaz took Ruth and she became his wife; and when he went in to her, the Lord gave her conception, and she bore a son. Then the women said to Naomi, "Blessed be the Lord, who has not left you this day without a close relative; and may his name be famous in Israel! And may he be to you a restorer of life and a nourisher of your old age; for your daughter-in-law, who loves you, who is better to you than seven sons, has borne him." Then Naomi took the child and laid him on her bosom, and became a nurse to him. [17] Also the neighbor women gave him a name, saying, "There is a son born to Naomi." And they called his name Obed. He is the father of Jesse, the father of David. (Ruth 4:13-17, NKJV)

Ruth's loyalty and faithfulness opened doors for her to the point where a simple woman, who was even a foreigner, became an ancestor of the Lord Jesus Himself. For those of you who serve pastors, your loyalty will bring you before great men and women. I have met and had access to certain people I otherwise would never have met, just because I have been loyal to my pastor. The loyalty I gave earned his trust, which then gave me access to some influential people in ministry.

There are many examples in the Bible of people who exhibited incredible loyalty. Let's look at the story of someone with one of the most-liked names, Ittai the Gittite. He was a native of Gath, a Philistine in the army of King David. His story is seen in the account of Absalom's rebellion in 2 Samuel. David had been king of Israel for many years, and unbeknownst to him, Absalom, his son, had been turning the hearts of the people away from him in order to overthrow his reign and steal the throne. Imagine the mighty, but aging, King David, his family, counselors, and loyal followers fleeing the palace to escape his son Absalom's murderous coup. Heartbroken, eyes downcast, and clothes torn in mourning, David stops in surprise when he sees Ittai the Gittite, a foreigner who had only recently arrived in Jerusalem, along with his family and servants.

> "'Why should you come along with us?' he asked. 'Go back and stay with King Absalom. You are a foreigner, an exile from your homeland. You came only yesterday. And today shall I make you wander about with us, when I do not know where I am going? Go back and take your countrymen. May kindness and faithfulness be with you.'" (2 Samuel 15:19-20 NIV)

This is where Ittai the Gittite shows what loyalty is by his response:

> "But Ittai replied to the king, 'As surely as the LORD lives, and as my lord the king lives, wherever my lord the king may be, whether it means life or death, there will your servant be." "Then David said to Ittai, 'Go ahead, march on.' So Ittai the Gittite marched on with all his men and the families that were with him." (2 Samuel 15:21-22 NIV)

The king urged him to return and not follow him, but Ittai was firm; he is the king's slave, and wherever his master goes he will go. Accordingly, David allows him to proceed. When the army was numbered and organized by David at Mahanaim, Ittai again appears, now in command of a third part of the force. He was a Philistine, but he was now in charge of a huge portion of David's army. Think about the position David was in as he leaves Jerusalem and how hard it must have been for those who loved him and followed him. He had lost his palace, and, to an extent, his role. He was pushed out of the work God had called him to do, and he lost the affection of his son as well as the support of some of his people. He was forced to leave his own city to save his life because of someone cut from his own cloth, Absalom. Yet Ittai, a foreigner, and the others remained faithful to David, and they stood by their word. What a faithful and loyal man!

Let's also look at the case of the three mighty men of David's army, Josheb, Eleazar, and Shammah. The Bible describes them as faithful men who were heavily credentialed after many conquests. Josheb, for example, had used a spear to singlehandedly defeat an 800-man army. Eleazar also challenged the Philistines, who had gathered for battle. When the Israelites fell back, he stood his ground and fought the Philistines until his hand was so cramped that he could not let go of his sword. He stood fighting alone until God gave him the victory. Even though he was at the point of exhaustion, he would not rest until the Lord brought victory.

The Bible goes on to say that after the battle was over, the Israelites returned to where Eleazar was and stripped the armor from the dead. So basically, he was left alone even when his kinsmen fled the battle, but he stayed steadfast and fought them until he won. Shammah also demonstrated such courage and won a mighty victory against the Philistines. Such were the caliber of the mighty men who surrounded David. The clarion call is still loudly ringing as the Lord looks for the Shammahs and Eleazars of today who will defend the faith and be willing to battle for the Kingdom.

A time came when David longed for water from the wells of Bethlehem, which was occupied by the Philistines then. The account follows:

> Once during the harvest, when David was at the cave of Adullam, the Philistine army was camped in the valley of Rephaim. The Three (who were among the Thirty—an elite group among David's fighting men) went down to meet him there. David was staying in the stronghold at the time, and a Philistine detachment had occupied the town of Bethlehem. David remarked longingly to his men, "Oh, how I would love some of that good water from the well by the gate in Bethlehem." So the Three broke through the Philistine lines, drew some water from the well by the gate in Bethlehem, and brought it back to David. But he refused to drink it. Instead, he poured it out as an offering to the Lord. "The Lord forbid that I should drink this!" he exclaimed. "This water is as precious as the blood of these men who risked their lives to bring it to me." So David did not drink it. (2 Samuel 23:13-17, NLT)

These mighty men risked their lives for the man they believed in. David whispered a wish that caught the ear of his faithful and loyal servants and moved them to action. They went into the enemy's camp to get some of this water, and they were willing to fight for what David wanted, no matter the cost. This is loyalty.

WHY YOUR LOYALTY IS IMPORTANT

As I have mentioned in other parts of this book, we are part of a very intricate plan of God in this world, to build His kingdom through various means, including his local church. The local church is not man's organization; it belongs to God, but He appoints a pastor to lead it toward a specific vision. For this plan to work and advance, God requires faithful and loyal people to plug into the vision of the local church. It is important to note that God cannot carry out His purposes Himself on Earth except through people.

Sometimes, what may be given to you to manage or take care of at your church may appear insignificant to you, but nothing we are involved in is too small. Nothing is insignificant or little when it comes to establishing God's kingdom. Look at the human body. It is intricate, complex, and yet every part plays a very important role, no matter its size. If one part remotely begins to dysfunction or totally shut down, the entire body feels the effects. It is the same with the body of Christ, of which we are a part.

Loyalty allows us to take the risk of predicting the actions and behavior of the people we trust. This is important for pursuing any vision. If you are loyal, it means you can be depended on, and no one has to keep an eye on whether you will discharge your duty or play your part in keeping a system going. The eye doesn't have to wonder if the ear is going to do its job or the if the feet will decide to be functional. Each part is resolutely loyal in discharging its duties.

> Look at the human body. It is intricate, complex, and yet every part plays a very important role, no matter its size.

I heard a story about a small group of people who came together on a farm owned by Billy Graham's father to pray for a crusade that was being planned in Charlotte, North Carolina. As Billy Graham was getting some hay for the farm mules, he heard the people praying behind a barn. He was a young teen then, baptized and raised in church, but had no relationship with God. One of the men in attendance, a salesman named Vernon Patterson, prayed that God would raise up someone from Charlotte to preach the Gospel to the ends of the earth. Later that year, Billy Graham attended a crusade in Charlotte where he felt convicted to go forward for the altar call. The rest is history. Who could have anticipated the impact of this simple prayer by a small group of people on a farm, committed to praying for the salvation of their city?

I have a personal creed I live by, which I wrote many years ago. A portion of it says that nothing I ever do is insignificant because it may help establish someone who may go on to become the next mountain-mover in the Kingdom. So, with this in mind, I give my all to whatever I get the chance to do. You have to stand in your place. If you are given an ushering role or a choir role, perform that role like it's your ticket to freedom! Why do we serve in the church as though we are doing someone a favor? I see it so often and it is quite baffling. For the many years I have served in church, I can't even count the number of times I have seen people gifted and called by God waltz their way into church, often late, to give off some coldhearted service. There are also some who promised to serve but vacated their positions when they got busy with their lives.

> Loyalty allows us to take the risk of predicting the actions and behavior of the people we trust.

Let's not forget the many people who wear their emotions on their sleeve so much that the slightest provocation causes them to stop serving, or worse still, leave the church. No loyalty. These are the same people who came in swearing allegiance to the vision and the pastor. Yet, they got upset when someone did something that didn't go over well. They vacate positions entrusted to them because of offense or basic of a lack of commitment.

> We appeal to you, dear brothers and sisters, to instruct those who are not in their place of battle. Be skilled at gently encouraging those who feel themselves

inadequate. Be faithful to stand your ground. (1 Thessalonians 5:14, TPT)

We are in a battle, but many have either not assumed or vacated their positions, with no understanding of what God has called them to. The scripture I have just quoted says to instruct those who have vacated their place of battle. If you vacate your position, you weaken and expose *your* team, and the vision is stalled. Loyalty and faithfulness are becoming harder to find in our churches. Most of the heavy lifting is done by 20 percent of the members at the most, and most of them are oversubscribed and burned out. Proverbs 20:6 RSV says, "Many a man proclaims his own loyalty, but who can find a faithful man?" The only way a pastor can accomplish what God called him to do is to have faithful and loyal people behind him or her. He certainly cannot do it alone.

About ten years ago, a magnificent Hindu temple was built in Lawrenceville, Georgia. It was constructed almost without generating any noise or significant environmental pollution. At that time, I was working for a company that oversaw construction projects in various parts of Atlanta. I remember many of my Hindu staff and those of the construction companies that worked on my projects take off for days and weeks to go volunteer and build the temple. Some even took a month off without pay. I asked one of them why they offered so much of their time to build the temple, and he said, "It's our pride to offer our time and money to see this temple built, no matter the cost." What struck me was the pride with which he spoke. This gentleman had taken a couple of weeks off to volunteer at the temple just because he felt it was his honor and responsibility. They gave free labor, money, time, and commitment to see the temple of worship built. All these individuals belonged to various Hindu temples spread across the state, yet their loyalty to their cause kept them together regardless of where they had come from. All they saw was the vision of

> Most of the heavy lifting is done by 20 percent of the members at the most, and most of them are oversubscribed and burnt out.

this magnificent temple being built. They were unified in their support and loyalty to this vision. I observed their commitment to their cause with such admiration and holy jealousy, if there is such a thing.

When you are loyal to your local church and pastor, you have essentially partnered with God to bring His purposes to pass. Loyalty is non-negotiable for every role we play in church. Your unwavering support and loyalty are the necessary fuel that provides safety to your pastor and the calming assurance of having a team behind him or her. Without this assurance of a loyal team, their focus and effectiveness will always be short-circuited, and hinder the progress of the vision.

If you have vacated your position of service, or simply not stayed loyal to your local church or pastor, there is no better time than now to make a change. The kingdom of God is waiting on you to fulfil your assignment.

THE MAN, HIS GOD, THE PEOPLE

"The strength of a family, like the strength of an army, is in its loyalty to each other."

— *Mario Puzo* —

O ur God is the God of process and order. His expected order for His church will never change, and He has already cautioned us to do all things decently and in order. Every pastor is caught in a heavy-duty tug of war, with God on one side and the people on the other. There is always a battle between walking in step with God as a leader and pastoring the people he or she has been called to lead.

One of the things I know my pastor has struggled with over the years is managing the expectations and pull of the people who constantly seek his attention. Being a visionary leader, he is focused on taking the organization in the direction of its vision by trying to raise mature people who can stand in their rightful place and help move the vision forward. At the same time, he is the general overseer of a vibrant church in Atlanta and exercises apostolic leadership over forty other churches who are part of the All Nations Church family and look to him to provide leadership, pastoral oversight, and direction. As if all this was not enough, he is the president of Advanced Life Inc., an organization he set up to train and teach others to pursue leadership excellence. Above all this, he is a husband and a father. Just think about what goes into managing all this effectively.

The many things I have just listed have to do mainly with horizonal relationship management and oversight. There was nothing in there about being a man of God and living up to his big title and calling. A pastor, a representative of God to God's people, is a daunting role by all accounts. Certainly, this role must have an overriding requirement to make time to develop and maintain the vertical relationship with the One he or she is representing. Herein lies the dilemma.

In Exodus 18:13-23, Jethro visited his son-in-law, Moses, after he had heard all that God had done for him and the people of Israel. During the visit, he observed something quite worrying, which he brought to Moses' attention. He realized his son-in-law was spending all his days managing the people's affairs, which was draining him. Let us read the account:

> The next day Moses took his place to judge the people. People were standing before him all day long, from morning to night. When Moses' father-in-law saw all that he was doing for the people, he said, "What's going on here? Why are you doing all this, and all by yourself, letting everybody line up before you from morning to night?" Moses said to his father-in-law, "Because the people come to me with questions about God. When something comes up, they come to me. I judge between a man and his neighbor and teach them God's laws and instructions."
>
> Moses' father-in-law said, "This is no way to go about it. You'll burn out, and the people right along with you. This is way too much for you—you can't do this alone. Now listen to me. Let me tell you how to do this so that

God will be in this with you. Be there for the people before God but let the matters of concern be presented to God. Your job is to teach them the rules and instructions, to show them how to live, what to do. And then you need to keep a sharp eye out for competent men—men who fear God, men of integrity, men who are incorruptible—and appoint them as leaders over groups organized by the thousand, by the hundred, by fifty, and by ten. They'll be responsible for the everyday work of judging among the people. They'll bring the hard cases to you, but in the routine cases they'll be the judges. They will share your load and that will make it easier for you. If you handle the work this way, you'll have the strength to carry out whatever God commands you, and the people in their settings will flourish also." (Exodus 18:13-23, MSG)

Moses had been commissioned by God to lead His children on an epic journey through the wilderness to the Promised Land. Jethro observed, however, that Moses was spending most of his time dealing with questions and concerns from God's people. The scripture says "… people were standing before him all day long, from morning to night." Basically, he spent most of his time counseling the people he was leading. They had been in captivity for 400 years, so freedom was a concept they had only dreamed about based on what their fathers had told them. So, their need for counseling was probably justified.

As a result, they came to Moses with lots of questions, which he spent his time attending to. He was doing a good thing, pastoring the flock, but that good thing was distracting him from what he really needed to focus on. He was on course to being burnt out, like so many pastors are today.

We as a congregation have hindered their much-needed vertical interaction with God, and have been content to restrict our pastors to horizontal interactions with us so they can deal with our life issues. Many times, it is because of our unwillingness to live up to the responsibility of growing up to deal with the challenges we face. We choose to dump all our problems on our pastors even when we know what to do to solve some of them. This can be draining on a pastor's strength, focus, and emotions. The Israelites in Exodus 18 loved it because what they most wanted was a pastor focused on giving them his attention. I am sure they somewhat had the interest of Moses at heart but their need for his attention was more important, regardless of the emotional and physical burden this activity brought him.

Jethro saved the day by giving Moses the template to the right kind of leadership. He knew Moses could not survive or be effective based on the model of leadership he was applying. What Jethro said was even more alarming: "Let me tell you how to do this so that God will be in this with you." This implies there is a model of leadership that appears effective and satisfactory but can create an environment where God will be absent. I dare say the day our churches release our pastors to be given to prayer, to the word, and to seeking God's face, we will see a marked change in our day-to-day experiences with God in our gatherings.

For a pastor to be effective in leading a church, he or she must have the assistance and support of competent men and women. Without this, the vision will most likely fail. The only person in the Bible who made significant progress without known support for a period of time was John the Baptist. Even he at a later time took on disciples who provided a support system. I use the scripture in Exodus 18 often when I visit churches to teach them about systems and operations. There is just so much to learn from it about effective organizational behavior.

THE BURNOUT MODEL

Having had the opportunity to travel and teach on church systems, I have often seen the lead pastor placed centrally as the engine of everything in the church, with people depending on him for everything from counseling to even the most basic decisions. They are just the go-to person for everything. He or she attends all meetings and all gatherings. This is certainly understandable if your church is in the early stage of growth, but if you are in a fairly established church and you still operate this way, then there is a problem.

There may be many reasons why churches operate this way, including a lack of dependable resources who commit faithfully to carrying a portion of the vision. This causes the leader or pastor to pick up the slack created by undependable team members. I have also seen situations where the pastor micromanages and chooses to be central to everything in the church, even though the roles have been assigned to dependable and committed people. But whatever the cause, this creates what I call the *hub-spoke model* where the pastor is the central engine to all moving parts in the ministry.

I have seen this model not only at the leadership level of the church, but even in departments where a leader is appointed over a group of volunteers to provide a particular service. The problem is this can never be a sustainable model or one that is conducive for growth and attracting others to volunteer and serve because leaders are unable to effectively delegate responsibility or create a system that is less dependent on them. Whether that is due to a lack of a proper system in place, committed volunteers, or just because they have a leadership style that is improper to the task of delegating responsibilities and managing a team, this model is ultimately draining on any leader.

Some people just have a need to be close to the pastor or expect to have directed, unfettered access to him or her. According to Ps. Brian Jones, "the 'close to the pastor syndrome' is a wonky dynamic where long-time members feel that for 'the church to feel like church' they need open, unfettered access to their pastor at all times." Ps. Jones also said that as churches grow, access to the pastor must diminish as the point leader shifts focus to pursuing a vision and raising up high-capacity leaders who can carry the load. Many churches fail to free their pastors to become leaders and instead tie them down with the expectations they had of their pastor when they were children.

For a significant period of time, this was the model in our church, even though we had outgrown the launch stage of the ministry. As more people were drawn to the ministry of my pastor, we grew as a church. We never had a shortage of people walking through our doors to join our fellowship. But we did not have the right systems to sustain our growth or effectively steer our efforts in the right direction to achieve our vision. Everyone wanted the pastor to bless their marriage, give advice on business decisions, referee a fight, provide counseling, dedicate their babies, visit them in the hospital, pray over their new cars, and bless their new homes.

The demand for his attention grew with the church until it became almost impossible to meet the demands on his time. He was providing counseling to people who could have solved their own problems with the points he gave in the last few messages he preached. In addition, our leadership team structure was quite similar to the hub spoke model I expounded earlier. Remember, my pastor provides oversight and leadership to multiple churches in various parts of the world and has to travel to spend time with them at various times of the year. Unfortunately, his role had been reduced to managing church affairs and counseling people, just like Moses in Exodus 18.

THE JETHRO MODEL

It became clear that a different path and system had to be chosen and implemented if we were going to be effective as an organization, capable of handling desired growth, and making sure our pastor was focused on the right things. Jethro provided Moses with lifesaving instructions, which later saw Moses achieving incredible feats in his leadership. Of course, it was not without challenges because he led a people who were fickle and still had Egypt inside them even though they were no longer physically there.

Jethro gave Moses three basic instructions:

- Find competent men and appoint them as leaders based on their individual capacity.
- Set up systems to make the church effective in handling its business.
- Seek God's face and teach the people.

Jethro knew it was important for Moses to separate himself from the daily drudgery of ministry and focus on seeking God's face so he could be more effective at providing the much-needed leadership. He told him to "be there" for the people before God. In other words, he was to give himself to intercession on behalf of the people and instruct them on how to live.

IDENTIFY COMPETENCE

Finding competent men is probably the greatest complaint pastors and leaders have. We have no one to help us. Even if we have some support, getting them committed enough to exhibit the level of dedication needed for the pastor to entrust leadership to can be a challenge. Moses was first asked to keep a sharp eye out for competent men who could help carry the load. I am a firm believer that God will always, without fail, send the right support to help anyone He has called or sent on a mission; and whom He sends, He makes provision for.

> You have to commit to identify, train, and raise competent people, people you know are prepared to run with you on your journey. Then pour yourself into training them. That takes time and commitment.

I have heard some tell my pastor that he is fortunate to

have someone like me serve under him and be committed to him all these years. But I always counter that statement by saying I never came to my pastor in this state of readiness to support the level of responsibility that has been entrusted to me now. Yes, I may have been competent enough to play an instrument, but it took the special eye of my pastor to identify me and hold on to me over the years regardless of the many times I failed. He must have seen more in me than I saw in myself.

Many times, the help needed to grow your vision is within your congregation, but it does not always come prepared or dressed for the occasion. The pastor is instructed to keep a sharp eye out for competent people. If competent people were always easy to identify, why would the Bible say to keep a sharp eye out to identify them? It means you have to look beyond what you see in the people you have. Don't write people off as ineffective based solely on what you see in them now. See them beyond their now. You have to commit to identify, train, and raise competent people, people you know are prepared to run with you on your journey. Then pour yourself into training them. That takes time and commitment. Also, don't pick people just like you or who appear to be a cultural fit for what you're trying to accomplish. If you're all the same on a team, chances are that multiple people will be redundant.

Some pastors mistakenly place a lot of expectations on the arrival of ready-made help. They expect to find that processed, trained, and already-exposed individual who comes into the ministry, ready to provide a much-needed service. While that could happen, it may take you a few months or years to find someone like that, or it may never happen at all. Of course, if you operate a model of paying for skilled help, then you will attract such people. But how sustainable is that for a church trying to grow?

Any church or organization that invests resources in raising leaders and unearthing talent from within will always have a bright future. I have seen some churches, for example, raise musicians out of their youth within six months of sustained training. Yes, it may cost some money, but it is far less expensive than paying weekly for "professionals" to provide those services. Unfortunately, this is what has fueled the transactional service ministry where people with talent market their services to pastors and churches because of the rising demand, which has in turn informed and changed our service culture.

When the instruction to keep a sharp eye out for competent people was given, competence was qualified. This is where the topic gets touchy. When Jethro told Moses to find competent people, he qualified the requirement by telling him to find:

- Men who fear God
- Men of integrity
- Men who are incorruptible

If you are a pastor with organizational leadership responsibilities, please stop appointing leaders based solely on skill, talent, and competence. Being good at playing an instrument does not make someone a leader. Being a good usher does not make someone a leader. Having a passion for the youth does not make someone a good youth leader. Talent and interest in a service do not mean an individual who is interested in that service will be able to oversee the group assigned to provide it.

Talent and skill can place someone in leadership and give him or her a voice of influence. But, if that is your basis for selecting and appointing leaders, then your teething problems might last longer than desired. It is important to provide mentoring and spiritual training to enable your leaders to grow in integrity and understanding of stewardship. Many people like to be appointed into leadership but lack the commitment and attitude to provide the required stewardship necessary to successfully lead a group. In other words, a person cannot seek to be in a leadership position without being committed to steward and produce the results required of good leadership.

According to Patricia Lotich, founder of Smart Church Management, there are ten key questions to consider when seeking to appoint people into church leadership. These are:

1. Are they committed to the mission of the church?
2. Do they demonstrate Godly character in every area of their lives?
3. Do they communicate effectively?
4. Do they have a teachable heart?
5. Are they flexible?
6. Are they team oriented?
7. Do they lead by example?
8. Do they demonstrate accountability?
9. Do they have influence within the membership?
10. Do they have a heart to serve?

She goes on to say that "Church leadership is about serving, and people appointed to positions of authority need to have a servant's heart and commitment to be part of the team that gets things done." The leader must have an unwavering commitment to the senior pastor and the vision, along with a demonstrated love for the people he or she has been called to lead. You will notice that none of the ten questions has anything to do with the description of a specific role or the ability to deliver a particular service. They do, however, describe the most important leadership qualities necessary in order to be called a leader.

The most important thing to understand is that your church members are your most important asset, and entrusting your most important assets to just anyone is not a wise decision. Be sure they have the qualities necessary to become the kind of leader who will satisfy all ten of those questions I have just listed, or be committed to train them to become that kind of leader.

SYSTEMS AND STRUCTURES

Jethro's next instruction to Moses was to appoint leaders over groups organized by the thousand, by the hundred, by fifty, and by ten. This indicates structure and systems to create an organization that is healthy on the inside. After all, what's the purpose in portraying wellness on the outside when all is not well within?

The systems that are created would enable the pastor to grow a church that is not dependent on his constant presence and attention. They would serve to group and organize the different functions of your organization so that everything gets done efficiently and well. Systems improve communication, establish accountability, reveal reporting structures, and eliminate chaos.

In setting up a system, you must ask yourself the following questions:

- How do you work within?
- How can you design processes to enable the sum of the different parts to move the organization in the right direction?
- How can you develop the best way to carry out the required functions within the organization so that the processes are repeatable and efficient regardless of who carries out the function?

First identify where you are and the gaps that need to be addressed. Next, define and document how you are going to work going forward. How are you training your members to ask for help? Carry out an honest self-analysis to identify any bottlenecks in your existing model and be bold to make the required changes that will bring traction to your progress. Clearly identify who is going to do what and who reports to whom. In summary, define accountability paths so that everyone knows what is expected of them. This is vital if you are to define order right from the onset.

Once you decide the direction of your organization or establish the vision, take inventory of all the functions your church needs to perform. Then group these into areas of responsibility and supervision. Next assign competent people who understand the function to lead. Everyone answers to someone. Organizational structures help make clear who answers to whom and where they fit in the chain of command.

Our church set up a system that empowered associate pastors and other specific offices to be responsible for managing the affairs of the people and the needs of the organization. We acquired business-minded people who were leading major corporations to bring their much-needed skills to help us set things right. We realized that growing an effective organization was totally different from the skillsets needed to pastor people, but not everything in church can be managed from a spiritual perspective. David brought in skilled men, not priests, to help build the temple.

When we started setting things right at our church, we felt the effects of the change after some time. We had the vision of setting up a system that was largely independent of our pastor's daily input and oversight, so he could be free to function in his leadership role as God designed him to do. Of course, this was not easy to pull off because change is not easy. Anytime you try to change a system, one that is set in its way of doing things, you will encounter resistance because it takes time to get buy-in from the constituents. For a time, you might even get resistance from the very people who are supposed to help make things work. Our church had leaders who were used to seeking the pastor directly for instruction and feedback. So when we introduced another individual who wasn't the senior pastor to fulfill that role, they resisted the change. Regardless of the opposition faced, however, it is important to keep pushing the agenda for a new system, or you will never succeed. Keep the team informed on why it is important to make the changes you are making. We constantly showed the team the importance of having a system that frees our pastor to attend to his apostolic duties and to enable him to lead us from the right position.

SEEK GOD'S FACE AND TEACH THE PEOPLE

The third instruction from Jethro to Moses was to focus on his most important role: to seek God's face and instruct the people. Your pastor is like the captain of a ship who steers it in the right direction from the bridge, using knowledge and data, and backed by the Holy Spirit. The role of your pastor is so critical to the growth of your church that it is paramount to create systems that limit distractions to what he or she is supposed to be focused on. I am not saying counseling and other forms of activities requiring pastoral input is a waste of time, but if you have a church of even twenty people, and everyone is depending on the pastor to help solve their problems, what time does he have left to lead from the front? This has been a dilemma for pastoral leadership forever.

> A church can never walk in power if the pastor is more focused on the horizontal than on the vertical requirements the position demands.

A pastor must be there for his or her people, but the more vital necessity is for the pastor to have the right support team around him or her in order to help offload some of the critical functions of the organization to able hands. If competent people are in the right positions, and are plugged into the vision, then progress is inevitable. This system would enable the pastor to spend time before God and provide a much-needed word to enable us to live better lives. A church can never walk in power if the pastor is more focused on the horizontal than on the vertical requirements the position demands. That puts the pastor in a continual tug of war, only he's the rope being pulled! Sometimes our desire to build our churches and pastor our people can override everything else so much that our churches stagnate spiritually, leading to what I call a corporate progress stall. If Jethro had not provided the much-needed strategy to realign Moses' focus, and free him from the burdens of the people, the entire vision of taking them to the Promised Land would have been in jeopardy.

Like us, they were going on a journey they had never been on before, and it needed a skilled and informed captain who was in touch with the One providing them with the directions on how to get there! The scariest part of Exodus 18 is that Jethro said, "let me tell you how to do this so that God will be in this with you." This implies that God was not in what Moses was doing before Jethro provided him with instruction, even though he was pastoring the people and providing counseling to them. I hope some leader or pastor will meditate on this for a while.

THE TREE ANALOGY

People are drawn to a pastor for various reasons, such as the quality of the teaching or for his or her charisma. But in my case, regardless of the stellar qualities of Pastor Frank, the one thing that overrides everything else is his heart for broken people. He knows and understands his calling to the broken and the wounded. I have seen him extend himself to so many people over the last twenty-five years that I have lost count of how many have found hope to live again, because of his ministry.

When you have a pastor whose heart is so full of compassion, it is even more pertinent for the team that surrounds him or her to be protective of the pastor because it is easy for others to become dependent on the pastor more than they should. To compensate for having less access to the pastor than the congregation is used to, the people who step in to provide the attention, counseling, and leadership the pastor once provided have to exhibit those same qualities the pastor exhibits.

The analogy of a tree can be used to demonstrate good systems. A tree has roots connected to a stem or trunk, branches, and leaves. The roots are in the ground to provide stability while drawing on nutrients from the ground. The stem and branches carry the nutrients to the leaves, which bear fruit in due season. The stem represents the pastor who carries the structure and maintains responsibility for supplying nutrients to the rest of the tree through its connection to the ground. The branches, which grow off the stem, represent those who surround the pastor. These are the people who bear the leaves, representing the congregation, that ultimately bear fruit if the right nutrients and support systems are in place. Branches look like smaller stems growing off the main stem. If the tree is to grow and bear fruit, it is important the branches carry the same nutrients the trunk carries. If, for some reason, the process of passing nutrients from the stem to the leaves gets broken, the leaves will eventually wither and die.

Consider the following observations drawn from this analogy:

- The branches (leaders) must reflect the essence and passion of the pastor in order to create a system that is independent of the pastor's daily involvement.
- A leader must be connected to the pastor if the leaves connected to it are to bear proper fruit.
- A leader must propagate the same message of the house just like a branch connected to a tree carries the same nutrients in the stem to the leaves. This demonstrates oneness of heart and vision.
- A healthy tree has leaves bearing beautiful flowers and fruit in due season. This means the glory of a church is always in engaged in the process of maturing and prospering the people within its fold.
- The leaders providing support are the ones who have closer contact with the congregation than the pastor does, just like the leaves are growing from and attached to the branches. Because

of this, your leaders have more access to the congregation and potentially more influence than the pastor.

- If the branches don't provide what the leaves need, the leaves will find a way to detach from the branches (the leaders) and get what they were getting directly from the pastor. Using our analogy, that would mean they would find a way to reattach and grow off the stem. In the natural world, that would obviously produce an abnormal tree.

In our churches, however, we often see members find a way to detach from established failing protocol and find a way to access the pastor because the branches (leaders) that are supposed to provide the essence they desire are ineffective.

To all the leaders who serve under a pastor to support the vision in the church, your inability to grow in place and reflect the appropriate leadership qualities will hinder the normal growth of your church. The very people whose thriving reflects the health and strength of your organization are the ones you will lose first in the winter season if you don't have the right systems in place.

CULTURE – YOUR KEY TO GROWING YOUR CHURCH

"The strongest force in an organization is
not vision or strategy – it is the culture which
holds all the other components."

— Sam Chand —

I have seen culture enable or hamper the growth of many organizations. Certainly, in our own church, we have fought this all-important battle of incubating and nurturing a culture that is conducive to achieve our vision. I strongly believe that culture can propel you to or hinder you from attaining your desired growth. One of my roles in our church is to help set up systems that help move the church toward our vision, but I constantly have to battle the difficulty to devising systems that nurture a culture conducive to achieving our vision. Michael Watkins said, "culture is an organization's immune system." Once your immune system is compromised, your body gets sick. In the same way, if your organizational culture is "sick," you are in trouble.

Having been in the corporate world my entire career, I have seen culture play out both positively and negatively depending on how it is allowed to develop and shape the organization. There were times when I witnessed a company deliberately implement systems that created a culture which then produced a level of synergy that left the employees speechless for all the right reasons. Productivity increased and the feel-good factor among the employees was simply one to envy.

So, what is culture? Michael D. Watkins defined culture as the *consistent, observable patterns of behavior in organizations*. It can also be defined as the environment or atmosphere in which your organization or church functions. Let's think about that for a moment: *it is the environment in which your church operates*. If atmosphere and environment can be created, then culture can be defined and implemented deliberately, by design. It is the defined or default values that create the environment within which your church operates, informing your members how things are done and how to behave. This is an incredible truth. The leaders of a church can define the value system of their church, implement it, and constantly enforce it through various methods. If your culture determines how people behave, then it directly affects your ability to achieve your goals and vision because vision is fully dependent on your people. So, if you create a culture where your people are not challenged to own and pursue the vision of the church, and all they think about is "What's in it for me?" this will result in a stunted church riddled with a consumer mentality.

Preaching alone will not grow your church. No, it won't. I am blessed to sit under one of the most dynamic preachers, but we realized after a while that good preaching coming from the pulpit without introducing other systemic measures that create an environment for our people to thrive in would result in a long, hard road toward our vision. I have had the opportunity to speak to multiple pastors and leaders both in the church and in the corporate world, and the question I get asked the most is how to get their people to embrace the vision and own it. Most of these leaders are dynamic preachers who can preach a storm when given the chance, but there appears to be a disconnect when it comes to knowing how to create an environment full of passionate people who are ardent contributors and producers, and not just consumers. My answer each time is culture.

In the early part of our ministry in London, we placed a lot of emphasis on "doing ministry," which meant doing all the things a typical church would do while depending heavily on the excellent ministry of our pastor, who never failed to deliver. But having a great pastor and preacher rarely translates into an excellent church, unless you have the right systems in place that leverages your pastor's influence and draw to create the right culture. We had a great pastor but there was a clear disconnect between his level of excellence and how the people around him handled ministry.

WHY CULTURE IS IMPORTANT

Culture will trump vision every time. It took me a while to accept this truth. I did not realize that until we were able to deliberately design the kind of culture we desired, the various groups within the church would compete to create a default culture. This resulting environment would drive our efforts either in the direction of our vision or further away from it. The environment you create, whether consciously or inadvertently, will always affect the behaviors and attitudes of the people you depend on to help you achieve the vision. Culture functions very much like the operating system of your church. It is what enables the software of your vision to run.

As an organization, your most important resource is your people—your human capital. Capital is an asset that allows an organization to make progress to further its goals. Human capital then is the sum total of your people's time, knowledge, skills, and other resources the organization can use to achieve its vision. Regardless of how good or compelling your vision is, you will still need to depend on your human capital to achieve it. Realizing that, you need to create a culture that is a capable of inducing

> Culture functions very much like the operating system of your church. It is what enables the software of your vision to run.

growth. I like to compare this with planting a seed. To provide the optimum chance for growth, you would plant the seed in good soil and ensure the environment is conducive to providing the needed growth. If you plant the seed in stones or place it in freshly poured concrete, it will die. If you plant it in dry soil and don't water it, or sometimes treat and aerate the soil, it may not germinate or thrive. Your vision to get a fully mature tree that thrives on its own is directly affected by the soil environment you plant the seed in. If the soil is not the kind that is ca-pable of inducing growth and development in the seed, then it doesn't matter how much water you pour on it; the seed will not germinate and grow. This is the importance of environment.

Let's use high school sports as another example. It is quite common to see one high school excel in a sport, win multiple championships, and establish complete dominance in that sport. Another school might exhibit similar characteristics but in a different sport. Still another just doesn't seem to achieve any level of dominance the other schools exhibit. Several factors can affect a school's ability to win consecutive champi-onships over time, but nothing comes close to creating an environment or culture where success is continually expected. Schools and teams that are able to win championships every year, even though the team keeps changing because the seniors move on to college, has a system that wins championships, irrespective of who the team is, within reason. The entire environment is designed to make every team member accept nothing less than a championship. One sure sign of a healthy culture is when you can constantly produce excellent results regardless of the personnel you have. Culture is contagious and your people catch the output of your culture, whatever it is.

Now let's look at three healthy cultures you need to develop in order to achieve your vision. These are all lessons I learned along the way, which I know will shed some light on why you may be experiencing stunted growth in your church.

A CULTURE OF EXCELLENCE

Excellence is what we repeatedly and positively do well. It is defined as continually being the best at what you do. Excellence attracts, which means the more you emphasize creating a culture of excellence, the more people you attract. Excellence also retains. When people join your church and you have a system created to maintain excellence, they will stay. Toxic and erratic cultures do not retain good people. You can have the most dynamic preacher who can draw many people to your church, but the culture and people you have can often be more powerful in determining whether people will stay. You can lay out a strong vision for your organization, but if you do not have the right culture, you will not make much progress.

Excellence starts at the top. It starts with a clearly defined vision and a definition of how things will be done within the church. If you miss this step, you will end up having a lot undo in the future. You cannot function as a boat on the seas without knowing where you're going because not every destination is a good one. The visionary must first have a core team that holds the vision and its execution plan dear. The leadership team must be sold out to the vision and committed to excellence. If you want punctuality to be a culture in your church, you must model and teach it consistently. The same holds true for every behavior you intend to see as a mainstay in your cultural makeup. The leader or pastor must sell the vision and define what excellence means. For our church, it meant consistent punctuality, innovative service delivery, clear communication, clear definition of roles, cleanliness, friendliness, as well as warmth and compassion. This is what I call the soul of the church. If the soul of the church is unhealthy, the vision will become like a hamster on a treadmill, a lot of activity but little to no results. When you culture is unhealthy, everything becomes a chore, resulting in a lack of energy within your team. This creates a system where people come to church just because of the pastor. They lose interest in service and in building relationships within the church. One of my favorite writers, Carey Nieuwhof, said, "If the culture is healthy, amazing things happen. People love being there. People grow. Great leaders come and stay. Your church becomes attractive to the community and more fully accomplishes its mission."

My pastor has preached on this issue countless times. We see this principle in the story of the Queen of Sheba, who heard of the excellence of King Solomon and decided to go and see it for herself. Excellence attracts people with even better skills and resources to come in to support the vision. I usually explain this principle when I get the chance to speak to various leaders and their support staff. As you grow in excellence and decide not to compromise your organizational values, you will attract people who often times have more to give than those you have. Assuming you have a clearly defined system of integrating new people into your team without causing any heartburn among those who started journey with you, these new people will help raise the level of excellence even higher, thereby attracting others who will be attracted to this new level of excellence. This process will keep repeating itself if you have the right systems in place. Excellence will bring in people you would otherwise not have reached. It will advertise your brand without you forcing it.

Building excellence takes time and effort. It takes commitment to do whatever it takes within reason to excel in all the qualities that will help you establish a progressive and supportive culture. You cannot go from Ground Zero to the heights of excellence in one day. Excellence is a journey that happens in stages. Your organization develops in stages and grows over time, along with the systems you create to support it. You can achieve excellence with the little you have, and at whatever stage of organizational development you're in. You just have to know what you want and be committed to creating the right environment to achieve it.

A Culture of External Focus

One of the basic errors I see in the Body of Christ is what I call the salt-shaker mentality. A lot of churches are just content to come to church and just "do church." They go to church, take part in the service, and then leave until the next service. These churches have become like salt stuck in a shaker with absolutely no engagement in their communities and without any knowledge of what the pertinent issues are. Every church is located in a community; that should be the first focus of attention. Instead, we become comfortable just being salt stuck in a shaker. This leads to excessive interaction with each other, and our concerns revolve around who is talking to or about whom. Real church is what happens Monday through Saturday and not what happens on a Sunday morning. Sunday mornings are just for refueling and recharging your internal batteries.

When you begin to see your church as your only community, you open yourself up to the danger of becoming insular. All you know as a community becomes your church. I am not saying building community within your church is wrong, but when all the community you know as an individual and as a church is each other, you become too comfortable within and lose sight of the importance of interacting with your community. What's the effectiveness of a church when it is cut off from the community it's supposed to serve?

It is imperative that you build a culture that focuses on engaging your community so you can become a resource for them. When we realized we needed to make changes in our church to become more community focused, we set up a team that focused entirely on developing strategies to integrate us into our community. They became an intel-gathering team that mingled with community leaders during public meetings. We visited the mayor and offered our church as a location the city could use free of charge for any meetings that needed a big facility. We also donated back-to-school items to those in need. Those actions were easy. The more difficult part was doing the hard work of changing the understanding of our people to begin to think externally. This is still a work in progress for us, but we are devising better systems that will enable our church to see our community-engagement efforts as critical to our integration into the community.

Maya Angelou once said that people don't care how much you know until they know how much you care. When people in your community know that you care about their wellbeing and are there to provide support, you won't even need to preach to them. Let your good works go ahead of you as a church and you will be amazed at the doors that will open into your community. There is nothing more beautiful than a church that is heavily embedded and has become a strong influence in its community.

I read about a church that adopted a very innovative approach to integrating into their community. They decided to cancel their midweek service at their church location and instead use that time to attend any public events organized by various sections of the community. They would serve at retirement homes or delinquent youth programs, and organize feeding programs, which provided a way for the community to eat breakfast once a week. These amazing efforts began to change the church members into producers and not just consumers who came to church to be pew warmers when they felt like it.

Jesus was once asked, "Who is my neighbor?" He answered by telling the story about a pagan Samaritan man who didn't believe in the God of the Old Testament but helped a man who had been attacked and lay dying. This good Samaritan demonstrated love in action for this injured man, who, in reality, represented the community around him. He went out of his way to interrupt his own journey and program just to help another man. Let us not be like the Pharisee or the priest who ignored the injured man just to keep in step with their own insular programs. There is a greater reward when we get out of our comfort zones to embrace and get our hands dirty with our communities. That is how we demonstrate the love of God. Times have changed, and the means by which we share our faith have also changed, but the communities surrounding us are still in need. Your church was placed in your injured community for a reason. Stop walking around it like the priest or the Pharisee did. Don't be so focused on reaching "the world" that you forget the world starts right outside your church door.

A Culture of Service

It is important to make your church members feel uncomfortable in a pew-warmer role. Instead create a culture that urges everyone to join a team and serve in some capacity. It is irresponsible as a church member not to be concerned with serving. Each week, multiple teams plan extensively for your church service long before you arrive in the pews. We all have an individual responsibility to serve. We are all part of an intricate plan of God, which never includes being a pew warmer.

It is important for the leaders to build a culture that consistently offers service opportunities and promotes the benefits of service. If you have been in church longer than a few months and all you do is sit and consume without seeking opportunities to serve, then you need to change your perception and attitude. It is important for the leaders to understand that our primary job is to equip the saints for the work of the ministry. Gathering for a good church service without raising up servants equipped for the work of the ministry is not beneficial. Let's read the following scripture:

> No prolonged infancies among us, please. We'll not tolerate babes in the woods, small children who are an easy mark for impostors. God wants us to grow up, to know the whole truth and tell it in love—like Christ in everything. We take our lead from Christ, who is the source of everything we do. (Ephesians 4:14-15, MSG)

You cannot remain a child by continuing to receive ministry and not step up to serve. If my pastor never preached another message to our church, we have still received enough word to make a mark in ministry. Church leaders are expected to raise servants who are equipped for ministry, and it is our individual responsibility to study and grow to show ourselves approved, as workmen who do not need to be ashamed or be ineffective. When you create a culture of service in your church, it becomes non-negotiable, the normal thing to do, your reasonable service. You will no longer have to coerce or force your members to serve, and your people will find a sense of purpose that is bigger than they are. A church that has successfully created a culture of service has created the expectation of putting your needs aside and stepping up to serve. It understands that true fulfilment in ministry comes through giving and not receiving.

When you create a culture of service, it is important for your entire team to embrace it. You cannot preach service and have your team leaders pick and choose who can serve. Yes, I agree not everyone can sing like a pro, but everyone can serve in some capacity in some ministry. Help those, who cannot sing, for example, to find another ministry to serve in. For some people, it takes a lot of effort to step up and make the commitment to serve, and if that effort is met with disdain or rejection, then that person can become a pew warmer and lose their desire to serve.

> Leaders in service-oriented cultures always cross-sell their departments and not just the department they oversee. This means every leader is more focused on recruiting volunteers for the church rather than for their specific department.

Leaders in service-oriented cultures always cross-sell their departments and not just recruit for the ones they oversee. This means every leader is more focused on recruiting volunteers for the church rather than for their specific ministry. In my corporate consulting job, I always advise my teams to cross-sell all our services as a company and not just the specific service they directly offer. That way, they have a better chance of growing our footprint within a client's organization. In the same way, let's focus on selling service in church rather than service in a specific department. Always outline the rewards of service always and enable everyone to think outside of themselves. I know people who have been battling disease but have woken up to come joyfully usher or serve in the parking lot. I know others who have lost jobs but will faithfully serve in the music ministry and sing their hearts out because they have found a purpose higher than themselves. They do these things knowing it is a privilege to be called to serve others.

I wish I had known all this during my earlier years in service. I could have made a greater difference. But thank God it is never too late to change course and do things the right way.

ORGANIZATIONAL SUB-CULTURES

Before I conclude this chapter, I would like to reiterate the importance of being intentional about designing and nurturing the kind of monolithic culture you want in your church or organization. I use the word "monolithic" because it is important to have everything aligned, moving in the same direction, and being "fed" by the culture you deliberately design. As I have mentioned, some type of culture will be present in your church whether you design it or not. It is present by default. As your church grows and becomes more diverse, however, it is important to be aware of sub-cultures. Sub-cultures form when a group within your church becomes influential enough through common experiences or identification to develop its own sets of shared values that are significant to them.

Sub-cultures may not necessarily be bad, but they can become a problem if there isn't sufficient overlap with the main organizational culture. People with shared values can migrate toward each other in any large organization in an effort to feel some sense of belonging. This is not wrong in itself. The problem begins when they get so attached to their group that they begin to form a sub-culture that does not support the main culture the leadership is trying to nurture. These subgroups can get so much into themselves that they begin to prioritize their time together over time they could use to volunteer at church.

Suddenly, you have a group of people within your organization that does things their own way. They are present but they do not support your vision. They hinge to your vision, not to support it, but to grow their own vision within your organization. This is not healthy for any church. I have seen this happen often during my time in service. At that point, the issue becomes a matter of which culture speaks the loudest and is more compelling. There is nothing worse than having strong undercurrents in your church that are moving in the opposite direction of where you want to go. It halts and hinders progress and gets your committed people weary.

Dealing with this issue takes some leadership finesse. It's important that people find their space within the place where they worship, but it is even more important that everything is done in alignment to the vision. Be intentional about creating the right culture that is supportive of converting consumers to producers, who seek nothing but to live for a cause greater than themselves.

HELP THE WOUNDED

"Never judge other people just because
they sin differently from you."
— *Anon.* —

C
ompassion for others is the cornerstone of our church, and I
have learnt over the years how important it is to God that we
bear each other up and not destroy others just because they
may be struggling with some character deficiency that we may not be
experiencing. When we read the recorded encounters of Jesus with other
people, it is striking how much compassion preceded Him and guided
His interactions. Through my years of being in church, I have seen so
many get so impatient with people when they appear not to meet some
moral standard of their own choosing. As a church, we are supposed
to be in the business of helping each other stand stronger and not to
despise them because they failed.

One of the greatest stories of compassion in the Bible is that of the
prodigal son. His story is detailed in the text that follows:

> Then He said: "A certain man had two sons. And the
> younger of them said to his father, 'Father, give me the
> portion of goods that falls to me.' So he divided to them
> his livelihood. And not many days after, the younger
> son gathered all together, journeyed to a far country,

and there wasted his possessions with prodigal living. But when he had spent all, there arose a severe famine in that land, and he began to be in want. Then he went and joined himself to a citizen of that country, and he sent him into his fields to feed swine. And he would gladly have filled his stomach with the pods that the swine ate, and no one gave him anything.

"But when he came to himself, he said, 'How many of my father's hired servants have bread enough and to spare, and I perish with hunger! I will arise and go to my father, and will say to him, "Father, I have sinned against heaven and before you, and I am no longer worthy to be called your son. Make me like one of your hired servants."'

"And he arose and came to his father. But when he was still a great way off, his father saw him and had compassion, and ran and fell on his neck and kissed him. And the son said to him, 'Father, I have sinned against heaven and in your sight, and am no longer worthy to be called your son.'

"But the father said to his servants, bring out the best robe and put it on him, and put a ring on his hand and sandals on his feet. And bring the fatted calf here and kill it and let us eat and be merry; for this my son was dead and is alive again; he was lost and is found.' And they began to be merry. Luke 15:11-24 (NKJV)

This younger son decided to get his inheritance before it was time for him to receive it and go live his life in some far-away country. He got his wish and lived frivolously, spending his inheritance on anything and everything. As a consequence of his careless living and a famine that arose in the land, he lost all his wealth and then had to figure out a way to survive. There he was, the son of a wealthy man, but he had made some rough choices that led him to lose all he had. As a consequence, he was forced to eat food that was given to pigs just to survive. But what I love about this story is the statement that the son "came to himself" and decided to go back to his father, who lovingly received him and restored him.

Many, if not all, of us have wandered afar off and lived however we wanted until God had mercy on us and restored us. The good news is God is still receiving His prodigal children back home every day. But because of how judgmental and rigid we have made our churches, the people who need to be restored are forced to wear a mask. Here in the days of COVID-19, we are forced to wear masks as a safety measure, but many of our churches have been forcing us to wear masks to hide our true condition. Many wounded among us dare not open up to receive the help they need because their efforts might be met with disdain and judgment. They have "come to themselves" and acknowledge they need help, but when they try to come to church, to a place where broken people are supposed to be "fixed," the same church becomes their biggest judge.

We are losing our own. We are losing the people we need to help us build stronger ministries, all because we won't show grace. I have seen this so many times and it really upsets me. Nestled in the middle of the Lord's prayer is the following:

> '...and forgive us our trespasses, as we forgive
> those who trespass against us,' (Matthew 6:12, KJV)

> Forgive us the wrongs we have done as we ourselves
> release forgiveness to those who have wronged us.
> (Matthew 6:12, TPT)

Our forgiveness and receipt of mercy are directly tied to our willingness to forgive and accept others regardless of what they have done. Who a person is must never be confused with what they do or have done. They are two totally different matters. There are people who have walked away from church never again to darken its doors because of the way they were treated. As I have said in other parts of this book, we are in partnership with God as He continues to execute His plan on Earth. Through that intricate plan, we were reconciled to God and then given the ministry of reconciliation.

> And God has made all things new, and reconciled us to himself, and given us the ministry of reconciling others to God. (2 Corinthians 5:18, TPT)

> The true identity of anyone must never be confused with their failures.

Once we are reconciled to God, our job is not to appoint ourselves as judges of other people's failures while hiding our own. The church is supposed to be a place where the broken can be open about their struggles and find acceptance. People shouldn't have to fear judgment or whisperings about their failures. Some have developed a strong foundation through discipleship in the early years of their faith and may therefore not be susceptible to certain more commonly frowned upon failures and weaknesses of others, but that does not make them their judges. We need everyone who God calls into our fold to come in without any apprehension. Some have been led by God into our churches, but we have run them off with our attitudes. A soul coming to church is serious business. It is part of the big plan and mystery of God, who brings certain people into our fold who have some specific gifting or calling to help us move to the next level in ministry. No one but God knows what the person who tries to join your church or department will become.

Church should never be a place where people who need to be reconciled with God refuse to come because they see our hypocrisy. There are many prodigal sons among us desperate to be reconciled, not only to the Father, but to the family they left. If we have received the ministry of reconciliation, then why do we create cultures where people fail? This is what leads to people wearing masks. So, many among us portray an image of wellness when in reality they are dying inside, scared to open up for fear of being judged.

In my own life and ministry, I have had multiple occasions to call it quits because of the level of gossip, suspicion, and just plain lies some people have expressed about me, as if they were perfect. The mere fact that I am still heavily involved in ministry today is a clear sign that I have a calling. If I had allowed the things I heard to get into my boat, I would have long sunk by now. The people you see serving in church don't do it because they are perfect. Far from it. Sometimes the service they give is their escape from the potential dangers they face outside the church. Service is the only thing that gives them a real sense of purpose and the strength to say "no" to the things that try to make them lose their focus and balance. These are some of the real issues people grapple with.

This is one reason I fully support the vision of my pastor. Many years ago, he made a statement that if you can show people you care, you will never lack a following. That is so true. If we as a church can focus on creating an inclusive and welcoming environment for the broken, how wonderful that would be. Jesus said in John 13:35 that our love for one another proves to the world that we are His disciples. Love is a demonstrated action of care, devotion, concern, and commitment to each other regardless of the flaws we carry. That is the charge we have been given. I am not condoning accepting careless living among us because we do have a responsibility to develop maturity, but certainly we have to find a way for the broken to feel comfortable among us.

The statistics about church and Christians in the days we live in are quite startling. In the last decade alone church attendance has dropped 18–20 percent while the search for answers to the meaning of life has increased. George Barna described the American church as a mile wide and an inch deep. We are focusing more and more on programs that generate lots of activity but are missing the essence of addressing some of these critical issues. When it comes to our millennials, for example, the statistics are even more concerning. A recent Gallup Poll shows that only 42 percent of millennials attend church with some level of regularity, which is the lowest generational percentage. I would bet that if we all focused on creating church cultures charged with true love for each other, we would see a reversal in these downward trends.

THE LAZARUS EXAMPLE

One other story in the Bible is the story of Lazarus, who is described in the Bible as the one whom Jesus loved. Lazarus, whose name comes from the Hebrew name Eleazar, which means "He, who God has helped", fell sick and eventually died. It's an intriguing story when you study the dynamics of when Jesus was informed about his friend's illness and how he delayed a couple of days before starting on his journey to see Lazarus. Unfortunately, Lazarus died and had been buried 4 days by the time Jesus arrived. After greeting the family, he asked to be taken to the tomb where his friend Lazarus was buried and asked that they roll away the stone that sealed the tomb.. Part of the account is detailed herein:

> Jesus said to her, "Did I not say to you that if you would believe you would see the glory of God?" Then they took away the stone from the place where the dead man was lying. And Jesus lifted up His eyes and said, "Father, I thank You that You have heard Me. And I know that You always hear Me, but because of the people who are standing by I said this, that they may believe that You sent Me." Now when He had said these things, He cried with a loud voice, "Lazarus, come forth!" And

he who had died came out bound hand and foot with graveclothes, and his face was wrapped with a cloth. Jesus said to them, "Loose him, and let him go. (John 11:43-44, NKJV)

Not many scriptures buttress my belief that we are in partnership with God in the execution of His plan for humanity like this one does. Jesus prayed and commanded Lazarus to come forth to the amazement of everyone gathered. Lazarus came forth but was still bound in his grave clothes. He was delivered from death but still came out bound. I used to wonder why he did not come out "fully delivered," leaping and jumping for joy. But the instruction Jesus gave when Lazarus came out of the tomb is still the instruction we have been given today: "Loose him and let him go!" It was the church's responsibility to complete the deliverance by carefully removing the grave clothes so Lazarus could be fully set free.

Today, we still have the same responsibility to help others out of their grave clothes. They may be smelling of mold, dampness, or the world, but we still have a responsibility to help them come out of their grave clothes and get better. Imagine if those gathered had focused on the smell that must have been on Lazarus or the fact that it may not have been a good idea to touch him because he had recently died. He would have been saved but unable to function among the church brethren because he was still bound. If there is any role that is even more necessary and needed in the church today, it is the ministry to help others out of their 'grave clothes' to enable them stand stronger and live again. This is what Jesus has entrusted in our hands.

Why would we even be surprised that someone who has just been delivered from 'death' still smells of the muskiness of the grave? Why would we shun someone who used to struggle with smoking just because he or she occasionally smells of smoke when he or she comes to church? Salvation does not magically take away our physical weaknesses and struggles. It provides a way to gain strength and resolve to be better.

May God forgive us for the souls we have lost just because we were not patient enough to help them through their struggles. Never mind the fact that those of us older members who are the supposed gatekeepers still have struggles ourselves. Church is a spiritual hospital that has the ability to help people become better over time. There has never been a magic formula that transforms people into saints overnight with no sinners' problems. Let us, therefore, be patient with people and have compassion on them as they journey in their process of being equipped for ministry.

There is so much distrust among Christians, and it is hurting the church. Read the Book of Acts and you will realize a direct link between the disciples' ability to work miracles and their unity. It is evident that the power of the church is rooted in its unity. When Jesus was praying for the church before His Ascension, He prayed for nothing but our unity, that we may be one and of one mind. Is it any wonder that is where we struggle the most? Is it any wonder that the church has lost so much power? Look at how the COVID-19 pandemic exposed the shallowness of many churches. I feel we are unprepared for even stranger times ahead of us. We must not relent in showing mercy to each other. We must not compromise on being a compassionate church that models the heart of Christ, for therein lies our power as a church.

What I like most about the Lazarus story is detailed in John 12:

> Now a great many of the Jews knew that He was there; and they came, not for Jesus' sake only, but that they might also see Lazarus, whom He had raised from the dead. (John12:9, NJKV)

> Word got out among the Jews that he was back in town. The people came to take a look, not only at Jesus but also at Lazarus, who had been raised from the dead. (John 12:9, MSG)

Suddenly people were not coming only to see Jesus; they were also coming to see the evidence of Lazarus who had been raised from the dead and delivered. His story had travelled far and wide, and now people were coming to see him to witness the testimony. This is church in practice, working with Jesus to continue His awesome work on earth. We have to break the walls that separate us as a church and begin to accept each other within our respective bodies. We have to be compassionate enough to help each other grow and get better. No one is perfect yet, and till we attain perfection, we will have many of us failing to meet a standard of Christian living.

If someone should happen to fail and you are fortunate enough not to be the one who did, please lend a genuine helping hand; for when it is in your power to do good, do not withhold it. . And while you help, do not let your right hand know what your left hand is doing. People are hurting and getting more hopeless every day as life gets more challenging. We have to be the church God wants us to be. Let us get out of our own way of becoming a stronger and more powerful church and stop judging and killing each other.

We will have to give an account one day of how we managed the work God assigned us. How did we treat that young lady who got pregnant? How did we treat that young man who struggled with smoking and drinking? How did we treat that lady who lost her husband and now has to take care of her children alone? Did we forget her and just go on with business as usual of having our exciting glitzy church services? Did we forget the youth who are struggling to make sense of our faith as they keep getting bombarded with new-age ideology? Did we shun the young man who is struggling with his sexuality or identity? Did we forget our neighbors who are struggling to have even the basic necessities of life in their homes? Did we do our best with all that God allowed us to encounter as His representatives on this side of Life? Selah.

SERVING GOD'S WAY

*"We will never change the world by going to church.
We will only change the world by being the church."*

— *Anon.* —

The foundation for the Christian faith is fundamentally based on giving. John 3:16 (NKJV), probably the most familiar verse in the Bible, begins with "For God so loved the world that He gave…." This establishes the fact that love is proven in giving. In like manner, 1 John 3:16 (NLT says, "We know what real love is because Jesus gave up his life for us. So we also ought to give up our lives for our brothers and sisters." The example Christ set is evident in His demonstration of Christian values. Amanda Thompson, a writer I recently found online, made a statement that lit up something inside me. She said, "A good measure of our spiritual health is our depth of concern for other people." She could not have said it better. A good measure of our increasing maturity in all things Christian is our willingness to give, serve, and be there for others. Each of us has been endowed with special gifts necessary for the building of God's church.

One of the errors in the body is the belief that we are saved to be served. When I think about the Kingdom of God, I see a complicated jigsaw puzzle where each part fits snugly into the other, which then produces a beautiful picture that is impossible to imagine if we only look at any individual piece. The entire gospel is a mystery that is impossible to understand with the natural mind. According to George Barna, the church is supposed to be the accumulation of people who take their cues from God, seeking to bring His vision for the universal church into reality. This implies that each person contributes some value to the aggregate outcome of the vision. The combination of skills, talents, spiritual gifts, life experiences, information, insights, relationships, tangible resources, and opportunities that God has allowed us to have provide the basis for our capacity to pursue His vision with unity and enthusiasm. If I carry out my role and responsibilities, you complete yours, and the other members of the body fulfill theirs, then we achieve good traction toward an expected spectacular end.

Service is the greatest barter system I have ever encountered. I believe God's word is so simple that we sometimes complicate it just to sound deep. Let's read Matthew 6:33 in the holy scriptures:

> ...and He will give you all you need from day to day if you live for Him and make the Kingdom of God your primary concern. (Matthew 6:33, NLT)

This is one of the most powerful and enlightening scriptures on what service means to God and should mean to you. The great benefit is God's promise to provide everything we need daily as we go about doing His business. This is what has consistently driven me in my service. I have gone to the altar of God and presented this scripture multiple times in my time of need. "God you said if I do my part, You will give me all I need from day to day...." Remember He has asked us in His word to remind Him of His word.

This is why I call it the greatest barter system. I serve *wholeheartedly*, making His business my primary concern, and in exchange, He works on my life and issues. This excites me. I am not presenting this as a "brownie-points" system where we do one thing and then God does something for us. He loves us more than that. But as we serve, He can't help but keep blessing and rewarding us more for all the work we put in to serve and bless others. He has promised in His word that He will never forget our labor of love. Now that's some promissory note from someone who cannot lie!

> For God is not unjust. He will not forget how hard you have worked for him and how you have shown your love to him by caring for other believers, as you still do. (Hebrews 6:10, NLT)

I love The Passion Translation even better! God continually remembers all you do in your service! He will not forget. Isn't this beautiful?

> For God, the Faithful One, is not unfair. How can He forget the work you have done for him? He remembers the love you demonstrate as you continually serve His beloved ones for the glory of His name. (Hebrews 6:10, TPT)

Remember, the singular thing that God prioritizes over everything else is His purpose, and He expects you and me to make it our primary concern. When you understand this truth, your attitude toward service will change. If what happens in the house of God becomes your primary concern, and you are sold out to playing your part in bringing His purpose to pass, then you could not be in a better position in God's eyes.

God can do anything, but He has chosen to use us to accomplish His purpose by doing what He has purposed for us. Making God's business our overriding concern means being available, responsive, and totally surrendered and sold out to Him. If something needs to be done, volunteer to get it done, without expecting a reward from man. If it lies in your ability to fulfill a need in the house of God, never wait to be asked. Never bargain your talent or service in exchange for a payment, favor, or recognition.

I have a question for you: what is God getting out of your life?

Think about that for a moment. Is whatever you are giving God through your service what He wants from you? Or are you just giving Him what you want out of the surplus of your time? We do not belong to ourselves. We belong to God. So, I ask again, what is God getting out of your life? What is the God-ward benefit of your position in Christ? It is critical that you serve with the right understanding. Remember that your service is part of an intricate plan of God for the advancement of His Kingdom. You are His partner! That's huge!

The church is riddled with too many people serving on their own terms. We have made it all about us. What's in it for me? If it doesn't suit me, then please accept my apologies. When I don't have a pressing need, I don't need God. Yet we are quick to quote scriptures like "I have been crucified with Christ; it is no longer I who live, but Christ lives in me; and the life which I now live in the flesh I live by faith in the Son of God, who loved me and gave Himself for me." Galatians 2:20 NKJV. We sing songs with deep lyrics like *I Give Myself Away* by William McDowell. If some of us understood the lyrics and the revelation in that song, we would certainly be demonstrating a deeper understanding of service. We sing songs like these all the time and yet fail to do what it promises or implies. Countless times I have seen people pledge to serve and be entrusted into positions that are key to help build the church but soon wane in commitment because they are too busy with other things or they just don't feel like serving anymore.

GET PLUGGED IN

When you get born again and find a good local church, your first step is to get plugged in. Finding a place to serve is critical to the advancement of God's purpose on Earth. Recognize there is a bigger purpose working behind the scenes. Your local church is your entry point into the purpose of God regarding the growth of His Kingdom and the revelation of His power and influence on Earth. So, get plugged in and make yourself useful to God.

Look at what the Message translation says in Ephesians 2:19-22:

> "That's plain enough, isn't it? You're no longer wandering exiles. This kingdom of faith is now your home country. You're no longer strangers or outsiders. You belong here, with as much right to the name Christian as anyone. God is building a home. He's using us all—irrespective of how we got here—in what He is building. He used the apostles and prophets for the foundation. Now He's using you, fitting you in brick by brick, stone by stone, with Christ Jesus as the cornerstone that holds all the parts together. We see it taking shape day after day—a holy temple built by God, all of us built into it, a temple in which God is quite at home."

This scripture clearly illustrates to me in basic terms what God is doing with us. His intention is to use us all to accomplish His divine purpose and to build His Kingdom. And there shall be no end to the increase in God's kingdom!

As a civil engineer, I have a good understanding of what it takes to build a house. When a bricklayer is laying bricks, he or she lays them lengthwise and in a staggered or overlapping pattern. This means that part of each brick lies on another brick and, at the same time, carries the weight of another brick in order to properly interlock and bond with the mortar that holds it all together. This pattern ensures effectiveness at maximizing the strength of the wall, by distributing the load and helping to resist lateral forces on the wall. If the bricks were laid directly on top of each other, the strength of the wall would be compromised, and the wall would not be able to resist the forces that are bound to act on it.

The purpose of God in building His house is for us to come together, interlock our individual gifts, support each other, and run with the singular purpose of achieving His corporate will for us. According to Ephesians 4:16, each of us has been given divine gifts necessary to the growth of all. So if you withhold your gift and refuse to deploy yourself in the kingdom, you shortchange more than just yourself.

For his "body" has been formed in his image and is closely joined together and constantly connected as one. And every member has been given divine gifts to contribute to the growth of all; and as these gifts operate effectively throughout the whole body, we are built up and made perfect in love. (Ephesians 4:16 TPT)

SERVICE UNPACKED

Throughout the Bible, we see many examples of what service in the kingdom of God means. We see a plan carefully woven by God, inspired by the Holy Spirit, and executed by men. The purposes and the plans of God have always been clearly orchestrated and executed in a fashion that defies human logic. We see God sending a baby into the world to buy back our redemption through a plan that was intricately woven into the story of the Old and New Testament. Study the genealogy of Jesus in the book of Matthew and the stories and prophecies that preceded His entry into time. This is what Paul describes as a mystery.

The Passion Translation provides a better understanding:

> And through the revelation of the Anointed One, He unveiled His secret desires to us—the hidden mystery of his long-range plan, which He was delighted to implement from the very beginning of time. And because of God's unfailing purpose, this detailed plan will reign supreme through every period of time until the fulfillment of all the ages finally reaches its climax—when God makes all things new in all of heaven and earth through Jesus Christ. (Ephesians 1:9-10, TPT)

This scripture states that "...because of God's UNFAILING purpose, His detailed plan will reign supreme...." Please hear me; the ONE thing God cares about the most is His purpose because it is the one thing everything revolves around. We just read that His purpose is unfailing. This is powerful! He crafted an intricate plan in which you and I have the opportunity to feature prominently in order to bring it to pass. This is why it is important to plug yourself into the purposes of God and make yourself indispensable to Him regardless of how small a role you play. Not everyone will become a Billy Graham, a T. D. Jakes or a Frank Ofosu-Appiah, but whatever our hands find to do, we are instructed to do it as unto God. His promise is clearly stated in the following scripture:

> "...and he will give you all you need from day to day if you live for him and make the Kingdom of God your primary concern." (Matthew 6:33, NLT)

When I caught this revelation as a young Christian, I made it part of my covenant with God. As I kept giving myself to His service, regardless of any challenge I was facing, it kept giving me access to God. I learnt very early in my ministry that if I commit myself to His purpose and allow Him to use me as He desires, that He would take care of the things that concern me. I bought into this truth hook, line, and sinker, and I have multiple testimonies that support this truth. God will never short-change you if you commit yourself to His purpose.

FIND YOUR PLACE

Being in the right place, under good God-led pastoral leadership, is critical to your destiny. When you find the right place to serve, you must become planted there. You have to be plugged into and be totally sold out to the vision of the house without ever unplugging or discharging yourself from your duties at any whim or offense. The purpose you signed up to support is bigger than your emotions. It is very difficult to serve in church if you wear your emotions on your sleeve.

Something happens in the lives of those who serve that does not easily happen in the lives of those who don't: they have a greater access to God. While God's servants still go through hard times, He makes Himself available to servants in ways that others don't see. God will still work in your life if you choose not to serve, but there are levels of access and blessings in life. The one who builds an altar of service will always have something to fall back on to negotiate with in times of trouble.

When I committed myself to join Living Springs International Church and serve under the leadership of my spiritual father, Pastor Frank Ofosu-Appiah, I gave everything. I committed to learn and improve myself in building a choir. I found mentors whom I pursued almost to a fault in order to learn something new every day. I was a broke student who had nothing. Sometimes I would struggle to have enough money to cover my weekly travel card costs to go to college during the week and church activities on the weekends. I lived off campus my entire time in college and needed to travel every day for classes. When I did not have enough money, I would always prioritize church over going to school. I would save the little money I had to buy a travel card to make it to church to teach the choir and play my instrument for worship.

Sometimes I would ask God to let someone bless me after the service so I would have enough money to purchase a weekly pass to go to school and honor my church commitments at the same time. But nothing would happen, and no one would give me a penny. Some would walk up to me and tell me how good the choir sounded and how grateful they were to have me around, yet I was struggling to have enough money to make it through each week. But through it all, God was training and processing me. I didn't need to expect anything from those I served; instead I needed to come to the place where I knew my help comes only from the Lord. True servants always go through processing, and that is not a pleasant experience.

Every day we had a service I would leave home early to get to church at least an hour before the service started to set up instruments and chairs. Remember we were in an empty rented facility that was being used by a small Caucasian church. We had to carry chairs from a storage building, set them up, lay cables for speakers, and set up instruments every day. By the time the service started, I would be sweating because of all the work we had to do beforehand. Once the service was over, we would tear down and move everything back to storage before heading home. This was my schedule for years, but I did it happily without ever complaining. I was just grateful to serve with other faithful men and women who teamed up to push the vision. You know who you are... may God remember you greatly.

Someone once asked me how I managed to always be on time to church every service day to do what was expected of me back then, considering I lived some distance away from church. I told him I calculated how long it took me to get to church based on where I lived and then I left home at the right time. I finished by saying with a smile, "It's just that simple!" Hopefully, he didn't think I was being rude.

In my early years in London, I didn't drive nor could I afford to own a car, so I depended completely on public transportation to make it to church. Regardless of the weather in London, I would take a train and transfer to a bus at least three times one way to get to church, while carrying a heavy 88-key piano to practice and prepare to teach the choir every weekend.

It was difficult to find part time jobs because all the available jobs required me to work evenings and weekends, which would have affected my church commitments. I was still determined to turn up at choir practice on Saturdays and church on Wednesdays and weekends. I had made the decision never to serve half-heartedly because I understood that I had entered into a service covenant with God. That meant service was a non-negotiable assignment for me, regardless of the personal cost.

THE STORY OF SAMUEL

One of the most riveting stories of service can be found in the book of Samuel. Samuel's story began with a barren woman, Hannah, who prayed earnestly that God would bless her with a child. The Bible says, "the Lord remembered her," (1 Samuel 1:19 NKJV) and she became pregnant. She named the baby Samuel, which means "the Lord hears." When the boy was weaned, Hannah presented him to God at Shiloh, in the care of Eli the high priest, thereby fulfilling a promise Hannah had made when she was praying for a child. She said, "Lord Almighty, if you will only look on your servant's misery and remember me, and not forget your servant but give her a son, then I will give him to the Lord for all the days of his life...." (1 Samuel 1:11 NIV).

1 Samuel 3:1 says that Samuel ministered to the Lord under Eli. Our service is always to God but under the leadership of His chosen and appointed leader. Your pastor represents God in your life.

In this narrative, we see Samuel sitting under Eli and serving with focus. He even encountered Eli's children, Hophni and Phinehas, and the debauchery and decadence they displayed. But in all this, he kept his focus, refusing to be distracted from the purpose for which he was serving in the house of the Lord. He refused to be contaminated by the culture the two brothers had created.

He kept honoring Eli even though many of the Israelites were not happy with him because of his children. Even God was not happy with Eli because he had failed to rein them in and correct their consistent errors. But Samuel understood, even at that young age, that he was chosen, and that his service was to God through Eli. And herein lies a very important lesson in service: our service in the house of God is to God first, *through an appointed leader.* This is very important to understand so that it informs your behavior and perceptions. It is also important to understand that any expectation for a reward or affirmation does not rest on a man. Then came Samuel's encounter with God, which opened the door to greatness for him.

> Then God called out, "Samuel, Samuel!", Samuel answered, "Yes? I'm here." Then he ran to Eli saying, "I heard you call. Here I am." Eli said, "I didn't call you. Go back to bed." And so he did. God called again, "Samuel, Samuel!" Samuel got up and went to Eli, "I heard you call. Here I am." Again Eli said, "Son, I didn't call you. Go back to bed." (This all happened before Samuel knew God for himself. It was before the revelation of God had been given to him personally.)
>
> God called again, "Samuel!"—the third time! Yet again Samuel got up and went to Eli, "Yes? I heard you call me. Here I am." That's when it dawned on Eli that God was calling the boy. So Eli directed Samuel, "Go back and lie down. If the voice calls again, say, 'Speak, God. I'm your servant, ready to listen.'" Samuel returned to his bed. Then God came and stood before him exactly as before, calling out, "Samuel! Samuel!" Samuel answered, "Speak. I'm your servant, ready to listen." (1 Samuel 3:4-10, MSG)

This scripture relays the encounter with God that Samuel had. He heard a voice calling him that sounded like the voice of his master, Eli. So, he would run to Eli only to hear Eli tell him that he didn't call him. Samuel ran to Eli three times, thinking Eli had called him, until finally Eli perceived that God was calling the boy.

> So Eli directed Samuel, "Go back and lie down. If the voice calls again, say, 'Speak, God. I'm your servant, ready to listen.' Samuel returned to his bed. Then God came and stood before him exactly as before, calling out, "Samuel! Samuel!" Samuel answered, "Speak. I'm your servant, ready to listen." (1 Samuel 3:9-10 MSG)

Samuel was available, present, and attentive. These are three key requirements for a sold-out posture. Being available is an internal disposition. Adopting it means you are accessible, dependable, and can be trusted to respond if your help is needed in some capacity. It means you do not choose what you'd do and what is beneath you. An available person can be used or obtained and be at another's disposal. Let that marinate for a minute.

Being present means having your focus, your attention, your thoughts, and your love all fixed on the task at hand, or what has been entrusted into your hands. If anyone is needed to respond to a need, you turn up. It means you understand that your presence is necessary to provide the needed support for growing a vision. Samuel was not distracted by the murmurings and challenges that existed within the church. He was ever present in the temple to serve and respond to any need. His sleeping area was adjacent to the temple and ever present. He took his service seriously. He was responsible for keeping the lamp of God burning at the right time until it ran out at night. Service requires your attention and presence. Supporting a vision requires your presence. If the church plans a program and you are a servant, you show up and support the vision with your presence.

The other requirement is to be attentive. This means you are ready to respond and act, to do whatever needs done, even without instruction, though you are always eager to receive instruction if given. Samuel was attentive to a call from Eli when he called. But one day he heard a call that sounded like Eli to him.

Many times, the voice of God will come to you through the voice of your pastor. Many times, when God speaking to you, the interpretation of the message or call may come through your "Eli." For those of you who have a call on your life, this is a good lesson. Be careful of how you treat your pastor when you believe you have heard the voice of God. Be very cautious. Never run off and start your own thing because you "heard a call." Abide by God's timing, for there is a time and season for every instruction you receive. As my pastor always says, the way you leave a place will determine how you enter your next level. Samuel honored Eli and continued to honor and serve him until his death. He knew of Eli's frailty and his inefficiencies, but he did not make that his business. He focused on what had been assigned to him. Period.

In my many years of serving under my pastor, I have encountered many people who would come pledging and promising the world to him. Then suddenly, just as smoke dissipates, they disappear, many times for no apparent reason. Other times, at the slightest apparent offense or delay in getting what they really want, they just move on. Like my pastor says, everyone wants to be a servant until they are treated like one.

THE POSTURE OF A SERVANT

When Jesus came to be among us, practically unrecognizable from His true divine and faultless identity, He humbled Himself and made Himself of no reputation as the following scripture says:

> Do nothing out of selfish ambition or vain conceit. Rather, in humility value others above yourselves, not looking to your own interests but each of you to the interests of the others. In your relationships with one another, have the same mindset as Christ Jesus: Who, being in very nature God, did not consider equality with God something to be used to his own advantage; rather, he made himself nothing by taking the very nature of

a servant, being made in human likeness. And being found in appearance as a man, he humbled himself by becoming obedient to death- even death on a cross! (Philippians 2:3-8, ESV)

The Passion Translation says it in even greater depth:

Be free from pride-filled opinions, for they will only harm your cherished unity. Don't allow self-promotion to hide in your hearts, but in authentic humility put others first and view others as more important than yourselves. Abandon every display of selfishness. Possess a greater concern for what matters to others instead of your own interests. And consider the example that Jesus, the Anointed One, has set before us. Let his mindset become your motivation. He existed in the form of God, yet He gave no thought to seizing equality with God as his supreme prize. Instead He emptied himself of His outward glory by reducing himself to the form of a lowly servant. He became human! He humbled Himself and became vulnerable, choosing to be revealed as a man and was obedient. He was a perfect example, even in His death—a criminal's death by crucifixion! (Philippians 2:3-8, TPT)

God lowered Himself and walked among us, becoming a man with fleshly patterns, humbled Himself to the point of washing the feet of His disciples, and subjected Himself to death on the cross. The same humility He exhibited on earth caused Him to ascend to heaven when His work was done.

Outside of Christ, my model of humility is my pastor. He is an accomplished man, sharp in the Spirit, flawless in character, a great communicator, one who has access to presidents and generals of our faith, and yet he makes himself available to the least among us. Many times, he goes to the church and spends time putting things right if something is amiss. He paints a picture of what it takes to serve regardless of who you are. In his words, the ground at the foot of the cross is always level.

When it comes to serving in the house of God, you have to see yourself as God's partner. Like I mentioned earlier, God has an intricate plan He has put in place, and He has enlisted partners like you and me to help bring it to pass. That's an honorable position to be in. The problem is, we see working in the church as removed or different from God's plans and purposes, even though they are directly related. I implore you to change the way you see service.

If you were told that serving in church is your only way to get a "ticket" to heaven, or if your purpose in life were directly tied to your service, would you change anything you're doing now? What would you change? How much more committed would you be? How much of a lifesaver would you begin to see your service? You must come to see your service in any capacity as an honor and a privilege.

WHAT'S IN IT FOR ME?

It's sad that we have made ourselves so important that the discipline of service is gradually eroding away. People who ought to be serving are still being served and even demand to be served. I have seen some who claim to love a God they cannot see and yet rudely refuse to follow the simple instruction of an usher. Some serve in departments but have absolutely no regard for the department leader they serve under. They serve because they want to please the pastor and not because they love the Kingdom. Such people are those who always get offended and leave when the pastor or department leader gets on their wrong side. If you've been in church longer than six months and you are still sitting in the pews, not serving or getting involved, but just consuming what is being served, then there is a problem.

Service is not about donating some extra surplus time you may have out of convenience, to chip in a little volunteering service once in a while. It is not something you do as a favor to the church. My heart aches when I see what has become of service in our churches. The few dependable people are being overloaded with responsibilities while the many others just sit to be served and criticize everything that happens in their church. It's as if they will serve and support the vision as long as they see a direct personal benefit and gain.

Why has service in church become so much of a what's-in-it-for-me thing? We are constantly almost begging members to rise up to serve and remain faithful to what has been committed into their hands. Why do we literally have to implore our own members to show up to support programs that have been put together to support no one but them?

Over the years I have been involved in the ministry, I have seen many trading their gifts for financial rewards and won't serve even in their home church until they can agree on a fee! When did we get here? How can you sit in your local church and have a skill that could help in some manner but refuse to serve unless you're asked or paid? Why would you know how to play an instrument but refuse to play in your own local church because you don't have time or because you want to get paid? One guy told me that he believes he needs to get paid because playing an instrument during worship service in his local church is very critical to the ministry.

When did the person who plays an instrument become more important than the person who constantly gives up her time to watch over the babies in the baby room or teach the youth during youth service? If the hand decided not to work because it believes it is more important and deserves more attention than the leg, what would the body do? Why do you think your own local church, which has given you a platform to keep pushing God's agenda on Earth, needs to pay you for giving you an opportunity to serve? If it is accepted within the culture and policies of your church to pay church workers, and it is affordable, then please go ahead. I have no issues with that. I am only addressing the cases where some refuse to serve unless they are compensated for their service. If you understood that you are God's partner in achieving His great plan, would you still adopt the same stance?

I am part of an online forum for musicians and I often see debates on musicians getting paid. In a recent heated debate one person asked why he can't get paid if the pastor is getting paid. In his opinion, he and the pastor are both ministering to the people, so if one gets paid, the other ought to get paid as well. I wasn't exactly sure what to make of that but to have the audacity to think you deserve financial compensation because the pastor gets paid depicts what service has come to.

When I remember how we were raised to serve in church, how we were happy just to be called part of the service team, never expecting anything in return but the honor of being given a place to serve, it makes me wonder how we got here. I also wonder why and on what basis we categorize certain aspects of service as more important than others to the point of associating those roles with financial compensation. What is the real motive for that? Some pastors have told me they don't have an option because the service providers have monetized their gifts and they simply have to pay them if they are to get them to serve in the church. This situation has held visionaries to ransom in some cases, forcing them to comply or be faced with not having enough people to serve on a Sunday morning.

There are many churches that have grown to a point where they willingly choose to hire external support or compensate some church workers for a specific service; and like I said earlier, I support that if it is affordable and is your vision. Paying some church workers was something we never did at our church for many years until we got a point where we decided to make a change. We had by then grown enough to accommodate it. But it took many years to get there. For some people, it is the job they do and so they go around marketing a specific skillset to get hired to serve in a church. That again is OK. But if you sit in your local church, fold your arms and refuse to serve unless you get paid, please repent. If you refuse to serve in your church or even support it with your attendance because you can't be bothered, please repent. The success of your church is dependent on you.

You have to catch a personal revelation of why you serve before you can serve in the right way and with the right motive. If you serve in church with the wrong motive, you will unfortunately miss out on all the opportunities and blessings that are associated with your service. Also, any whim or offence can make you give up your position and leave the body weakened. In 2 Chronicles 2:5, we see Solomon determine to build a temple for God out of the best of everything he could find and give, because he had a revelation of the greatness of God. If revelation undergirds your service, your posture and attitude will always be better. If you understand that your service is to God, and He has "partnered" with you to establish His kingdom, you certainly will not try to charge your church to use the gift that God gave you. You will understand that it is a privilege even to have the opportunity to serve in the house of God or be called to support your pastor in any capacity.

Privilege is a special right, advantage, or immunity granted or available only to a particular person or group. It is granted to you to be able to accomplish something or occupy a role with your unique gift. It is never your right. God needs you to do His work, but He can also raise many more "yous" to play that same role. Never forget that. If He found someone

> If revelation undergirds your service, your posture and attitude will always be better.

like me, and entrusted certain functions into my hands, then of course, he could find even better people to do what I am doing. It is only by grace that I occupy the position with which I have been entrusted. So I dare not serve with pride because of some overexaggerated opinion of my importance to the church I am called to serve.

Serve in humility, with the understanding that it is a privilege and an honor to be called to do anything in God's house. Be grateful for the opportunity to serve because it gives you the chance to build an altar that will speak for you and your children in the future. Serve even if the time may not be the most suitable for you, or even if you are "limping" with a weakness. If you think all the many people who come to church, dressed nicely, don't have a weakness or a struggle, you are sadly mistaken. Everyone has issues, and that's the common denominator for all of us in church. By all means, work on yourself to be better, and keep running regardless of the limp, or you will never serve.

Sometimes I envy the Buddhists and Muslims I know, because of their commitment and selflessness to their faith. I see a selflessness among them that I often don't see among Christians. They give their all whether it feels good or not. They simply count it a privilege to be able to be part of their faith. I have not seen any two of them fight or charge their local house of faith for anything they do. They don't even have the flashy things we use in our beautiful houses of worship, and yet not many on our side show devotion to our faith anywhere close to these brothers and sisters.

SERVING WHILE FLICKERING

Like the lamp that flickered in the temple that Samuel served in, so do all of us flicker. Some may burn brighter, but if our lamps were put in a dark room, we would see how much we all flicker. No one you see in church is perfect. If we are honest with ourselves, all of us have something that makes us bow our heads in shame. Unfortunately, for the most part, the church has become intolerant of people failing or falling into sin. The very place from which we are supposed to get help is the very place we pretend to have wholeness because we can't afford to

> If you think all the many people who come to church, dressed nicely, don't have a weakness or a struggle, you are sadly mistaken. Everyone has issues, and that's the common denominator for all of us in church.

be seen as weak. I am not advocating sin or taking the grace of God for granted, but there is so little mercy in church. So many people with a limp, a weakness, or an embarrassing incident that is eating them up cannot ask for balm in the house of God because those who are supposed to administer the balm have become the chief judges and gatekeepers to the corridors of Grace.

Have I been perfect the entire 30 years I've served in church? Absolutely not. Have I made some hair-scratching decisions? Many times, yet through it all, I have grown better and stronger. But I still remember how difficult it was for me to get help when it felt like I was just stumbling through what appeared as dimly-lit corridors of ministry. I remember the gossip and the attitude I experienced from the people I thought should have been the first to help me. Some of the very people I expected to help me grow in the things of God were the first to cast stones when I made a mistake. When I moved from London to Atlanta, one leader I looked up to travelled from London to Atlanta to tell members of my local church that I am not a good person. I still get chills when I remember some of the things I went through when I was growing up in the things of God and dealing with the downward pull of my humanity. Times when all I needed was help and not judgment.

There are many of you reading this book who have left your local church because of how you were treated when you joined or when you made a mistake. You never felt welcome and some may have heard rumors and gossiped about you. Don't let such people make you leave a good place because of their immaturity. They are not worth it. Church is a congregation of people who have one thing in common: inconsistency. You cannot let someone who has a character flaw make you leave a place that is supposed to bless you. If I had allowed my detractors to get to me, I would have missed out on many good things that subsequently came my way because I stayed focused and refused to let those who didn't like me win.

Remember the story of Lazarus in John 11 where he was raised from the dead after being dead four days:

> Then Jesus, again groaning in Himself, came to the tomb. It was a cave, and a stone lay against it. Jesus said, "Take away the stone." Martha, the sister of him who was dead, said to Him, "Lord, by this time there is a stench, for he has been dead four days." Jesus said to her, "Did I not say to you that if you would believe you would see the glory of God?" Then they took away the stone from the place where the dead man was lying. And Jesus lifted up His eyes and said, "Father, I thank You that You have heard Me. And I know that You always hear Me, but because of the people who are standing by I said this, that they may believe that You sent Me." Now when He had said these things, He cried with a loud voice, "Lazarus, come forth!" And he who had died came out bound hand and foot with graveclothes, and his face was wrapped with a cloth. Jesus said to them, "Loose him, and let him go." (John 11:38-44, NKJV)

One of the most poignant statements Jesus ever made is in the last verse. After Lazarus came out of the tomb, Jesus turned and told the people there to "loose him and let him go." This is the first responsibility of every Christian, to get into the trenches, help restore people, and nurture them to a place of wellness and maturity. I find it fascinating that when God brings people to our churches, we immediately set these high expectations of them, even to the point of looking at them through the eyes of suspicion, because they may not look like us.

Many around us are wearing their grave clothes and need someone to help unwrap them and set them free. But because they are afraid they will be judged, they wear other clothing on top of their grave clothes and walk among us, portraying wellness while bound. This is a major problem. We are losing people who could have turned out to be our local champions and the help we needed to move the ministry forward, if we had only had a little love and patience to nurture them out of their inconsistencies. I look at how I have personally grown to become relevant to the ministry, and I shudder to think what would have happened if God had not sent me my pastor and other people who subsequently stood beside me as key supporters when I needed someone to hold my hand and help me wade through the waters. Some may say I am advocating that people in our churches live any way they want. Far from it. I am appealing to the mercy and love we are supposed to shower on those who got out of the furnace a little too early and are not as mature as we may expect them to be. Never mind the fact that you yourself did not turn out 'well-done' in all aspects of your character.

I fully see the church as a hospital, which must cater to the broken and those who, through some weakness, find themselves disqualified by the system that ought to be helping them get better. And it is insane of us to go to a hospital and not expect to see sick people there.

THE 401K PRINCIPLE

Many of you are familiar with the retirement plan that lets you set aside money from your paycheck into a 401(k) account and invest it in the market. The idea is the value of the stocks and bonds you invest in go up over the years you are working, leaving you with a cushion of cash to use when you retire. My wife and I have always compared service to a 401(k) plan because our service today accumulates a favor and a return for our future, which we can't generate on our own. God has said in His word that our labor of love will always work for us in our future. There is no good we do today which does not come back to us in your future. I firmly believe this truth. This is why I seek to maximize every opportunity to do good that life brings my way. Colossians 3:24 (NIV) says:

"...knowing that from the Lord you will receive the reward of the inheritance. It is the Lord Christ whom you serve."

I am a firm believer that as we keep serving, our accounts are continually credited. Works before salvation is useless but I totally believe that works after salvation is definitely necessary. What we do with what Christ has given us is totally relevant. There is an expectation on us to play our part in the big plans of God. As you serve, you build an altar which you will need one day. The days will come when we may need to cash out on the 401(k) service we have given. Be very sure that you have invested in your account so you can go to it for a withdrawal.

THE WORK OF THE LORD VS. THE LORD OF THE WORK

If there is one thing, I wish above all else you would take from this book, it is the absolute importance of knowing the Lord of the work more than the work of the Lord. Many get so bogged down with carrying out multiple activities in church that they hardly have any time to feed themselves spiritually so they may grow. We unfortunately get to the point where we erroneously deceive ourselves to think that working in church implies knowing or being close to Christ. Working and serving in church does not make you a mature Christian. Your local church normally provides resources to help you pursue spiritual growth, but it's your responsibility to actively take advantage of those resources to grow spiritually. You can be in a church charged with good preaching, great worship and discipleship classes, but if you spend your time always organizing these programs but make no time to withdraw and feed yourself, you will not last.

I remember finding myself in this situation a number of times because of how busy I was with the "things of God", actively serving but making no time to even read my Bible or pray. I would go months without being aware I was even doing that. I would be busy walking around church discharging my duties but be spiritually dry like a piece of wood. No one knew it.

I am not alone. This is a very common state of a lot of volunteers who serve in church. They do so much to support the vision but somehow end up losing out on the most important thing – their relationship with God. Do not let your service in church become more important or bigger than the need for you to grow spiritually. Your service in church will for the most part take out of you. You give when you serve, and if you keep giving without replenishing, you will run dry. You need to supplement your service with activities that fill you up. Read your Bible, pray, have quiet moments alone with God, find someone to be spiritually accountable to and take time off to rest and recharge.

This is one reason why we have so much strife and issues in some of our churches. We get so empty and dry while serving that we begin to exhibit attitudes we ought to have grown out of. This results in having people who are ultra-emotional and get upset at the slightest offence. If you find yourself getting irritable at the slightest provocation and the work you do in church becomes a drudgery, it is usually a sign of spiritual dryness. It's time to take a break and concentrate on what is needful – His Presence.

Whatever it takes, prioritize your relationship with God over everything else you do. Do not confuse your service and busyness in church to indicate a closeness with God. The two are totally different.

The good thing is, when you spend time building yourself up spiritually, you will be even more effective in your service. You will find more strength and joy while you serve.

Plan to spend time in God's presence so you may grow in the things of God.

TEN LESSONS FOR SERVANTS

"In the end, the number of prayers we say may
contribute to our happiness, but the number of prayers
we answer may be of even greater importance."
— *Dieter F. Uchtdorf* —

LESSON 1 – COUNT THE COST

I t is important to count the cost before embarking on any endeavor. Many times we are quick to make commitments but slow to keep them once the feeling of the moment ebbs. Jesus spoke of the cost of discipleship in Luke 14:28: "For which of you, desiring to build a tower, does not first sit down and count the cost, whether he has enough to complete it?" The Passion Translation puts it this way: "So don't follow me without considering what it will cost you. For who would construct a house before first sitting down to estimate the cost to complete it?"

The decision to serve in church or anywhere for that matter, should always be done willingly, having counted the cost of what it takes to be dependable, available, and reliable. I have seen too many members respond to an altar call or pledge to serve a particular group or activity, but their enthusiasm wanes or waxes cool, and soon they are nowhere to be found.

Service costs more than just showing up as a church member. When you commit to serve, you have signed up and pledged to be dependable and faithful in carrying out a particular duty. You are in essence saying, "I got this." Never make a decision to serve out of emotion, or even out of motivation because someone preached a message that woke something up in you. Basing your decision to serve on some external influence will invariably cause you to resort to your "normal" when you no longer feel the motivation or the emotion that made you commit to serve. Every external influence that makes you commit to do something will always fade away after a short while. This is why it is important to base your decision to serve on an understanding that makes you commit to an endeavor. The understanding I am talking about is what leads you to count the cost of your commitment. It is the same thing that makes you focus on staying in your position even when unfavorable times come, or you don't feel like serving anymore.

When I committed to serve under my pastor, I did not give myself room to change my mind. There was no Plan B. I did not give myself a way out if, for some reason, my expectations were not met or if I found out the Hophni and Phinehas syndrome existed in the church I had just joined. When you join a department to serve, you will always realize that what you encounter is different from what you anticipated. This applies everywhere. You join a company to work and then realize the culture is not what you expected. You join a choir and then decide to stop because the choristers are not nice, or you don't believe you fit in. But when you made the commitment to join, you made it independent of these external influences. So why are you now deciding to go against your decision to serve because of other people or because of how you feel?

I have encountered unfavorable situations or people too many times to count. I have met countless people I would rather not serve in the same ministry with, but I found those feelings and situations irrelevant when compared to the benefits of my decision to serve and to be there for my pastor. Deciding to join a department to serve is easy, but when you actually start serving, it takes a head decision and not an emotional commitment to keep you committed. A commitment based on emotion will always be affected by how you feel.

Always count the cost of service, and do not ever think it will be an easy ride. If you're committed to the cause, you will always thrive in the office you've been called to serve in.

LESSON 2 – NEVER JUDGE PEOPLE

One of the first lessons I learned early in ministry was never to judge anyone I encountered because we are all running a different race. When the announcement was made that I would become the music director in our London church, and that I would be starting a choir that would lead worship and minister effectively, a significant number of people came to join. We started the choir with about 40 people. Of course, not everyone was necessarily skilled at singing or playing their instrument, but at least they had the passion and were prepared to commit to be trained. One of those who joined was an incredibly skilled drummer, a gentleman old enough to be my father, who had spent years touring with professional musicians. He was a humble and friendly, but he was also a chain smoker and loved to drink. He would almost always come to rehearsals smelling of cigarettes and alcohol. But irrespective of the physical state he was in, he would play the drums excellently, without error. I guess he was always in the "Spirit." None of the other drummers came close to him in experience or musical understanding. It never took much to explain what you wanted him to play in a song.

Regardless of his admirable musical skills, I found it difficult to work with him because of his drinking and smoking problem. I remember complaining a couple of times about this to my pastor. I told Pastor Frank that I couldn't work with the drummer because of his obvious problems. In my estimation, it was an embarrassment to be in his position and turn up at church in his condition. But my pastor looked at me one day and said calmly that I should be patient with people, because everyone has their personal struggle. I was a young fiery holier-than-thou boy with absolutely zero understanding of what it took to lead people. I accepted it but didn't agree with him. In fact, I despised the situation, and the drummer. Isn't it funny how we are so wired to judge others by their actions, but we judge ourselves by our motives?

During the first few weeks of the choir, I remember calling for a half-day prayer retreat, which was held on our rented premises. All the team members showed up to pray for the new choir and the strength to build it. We were in a medium-sized hall with over 40 people walking around and praying to the topics I called over time. As I led the meeting, walking through the crowd, I had a strange encounter.

I happened to walk past the drummer, who seemed intensely focused on his prayers. He was praying audibly so I could hear him as I slowly walked past him. He was pleading with God to help him overcome his drinking and smoking habits. He said it was embarrassing for him because everyone could see and smell his struggle when they came close. He was at the point of tears, praying for God to help him. I had never heard a prayer so genuine from someone with a struggle. His prayer caused me to freeze and feel incredibly convicted of my earlier indignation. Suddenly, I realized that it was not his condition I was concerned about, but his association with us. My struggle up until that point was based more on how bad he made us look to the outside world.

I suddenly felt ashamed because of the thoughts I had in me concerning his involvement with the music team. There I was, judging someone's visible struggle and forgetting that I had struggles too; mine were just not as visible as his. Nevertheless, I felt I could judge because I had categorized sin in my head and decided that sin is a problem only when it is visible. It struck me that every one of us in the room had struggles too; they were just hidden. So, I had believed in my head that it was cool to serve as long as you could hide your struggle or sin. I went home that day feeling terrible, but repentant. This was a tough lesson to learn. It cut me deeply, and though it's been over 25 years since this occurred, I can still remember the encounter like it happened yesterday.

I also remember a situation where one lady asked to speak with me in private because she had a matter to discuss. I asked her to call me later that evening. During the conversation, she said she was struggling under a lot a of guilt and fear because she had slept with a guy out of frustration and her cycle was four days late. She went on to say she was very disappointed in herself and even more scared of what others, including her parents, would think of her. Of course, this was a very tense conversation as she poured out her fears, contemplating the shame she might have to endure if she was indeed pregnant. I told her to give it time since her cycle could have been affected by other factors. I prayed with her and hung up the phone.

The next day she texted to say, "Still no sign," sounding more frantic even in the text. Four days after our conversation, she texted to say her cycle had finally come. Of course, I was happy for her that she did not have to go through all her anticipated fears, but more importantly, that she had learned her lesson to act wiser in the future. Then she said something that struck me: "Thank you for not judging me when I shared this with you." She also said, "Not even once did you ask me why I did what I did, but all you did was listen, pray with me, and hope the best for me." I made a very simple statement to her that I know she will never forget: "Go and do likewise."

Anyone who does wrong knows it and doesn't need anyone to hammer their mistakes home to make them feel worse. When I was dealing with this lady, not once did I ask her why she did what she did. It was clear that she was already repentant and had learnt a lesson. She just needed someone trustworthy to talk to. Rather than judging others, give them a hand to help them up. Everyone you meet in your Christian community is at a different stage of his or her walk in the faith. Be patient with people and love everyone. Never judge others because they sin differently from you. Everyone has their "thing" that makes them do things they are not proud of. I have realized that people who are quick to judge others have always been more guilty than the accused. Learn to be accepting of people and never become their judge because all of us are susceptible to falling miserably if a particular set of circumstances were created for us.

LESSON 3 – HAVE COMPASSION

One of the most fascinating stories in the Bible is recounted in Mark 5:1-18 where Jesus encountered a troubled man who was demon-possessed and out of control. Jesus had just finished a long day of ministering to a multitude of people in Capernaum and He was tired. He said to His disciples, "...let us go over to the other side." While they were in a boat, on their way to the other side, a strong storm arose on the sea, which generated a lot of fear in the disciples. While the storm was raging, Jesus was in the stern, asleep on a pillow. The disciples woke him up and He rebuked the storm. Immediately the wind ceased and there was a great calm. The disciples were so stunned by what they had just witnessed that "...they feared exceedingly, and said to one another, 'Who can this be, that even the wind and the sea obey Him!'" Now let us read what ensued:

> Then they came to the other side of the sea, to the coun-
> try of the Gadarenes. And when He had come out of
> the boat, immediately there met Him out of the tombs
> a man with an unclean spirit, who had his dwelling
> among the tombs; and no one could bind him, not even
> with chains, because he had often been bound with
> shackles and chains. And the chains had been pulled
> apart by him, and the shackles broken in pieces; neither
> could anyone tame him. And always, night and day, he

was in the mountains and in the tombs, crying out and cutting himself with stones. When he saw Jesus from afar, he ran and worshiped Him. And he cried out with a loud voice and said, "What have I to do with You, Jesus, Son of the Most High God? I implore You by God that You do not torment me." For He said to him, "Come out of the man, unclean spirit!" (Mark 5:1-8, NKJV)

I had always wondered why Jesus decided to go through this storm just to come and attend to a man who was so far gone that men had given up on him. It had to be compassion. It is in this passage that Jesus modeled how far He would go to reach a person that no one would have thought of, just to demonstrate the compassion He expects us to model. The text I just quoted says "when he saw Jesus from afar, he ran and worshiped Him." He ran toward Jesus and worshiped Him. This broken and tormented man called Him the Son of God at a time when even Jesus' disciples did not fully appreciate or know who He was. Fast forward to Mark 8:29, and that's when Peter responded with, "You are the Christ." Even then, some of the disciples still had doubts about who Jesus was until after the resurrection, yet a forsaken and tormented man knew exactly who Jesus was. Many times, we find such people in our midst, battered by life and abandoned by the church because we deem them a lost cause. But Jesus made a loud-and-clear statement by his actions that no one is forgotten by Him.

Outside the examples in the Bible about compassion, I know no other person apart from my pastor who has such a heart. He would move heaven and earth just to demonstrate love to anyone in need. In fact, he demonstrates compassion so much that I have often wondered why he would do that to someone who betrayed him or let him down. It is no wonder the vision for the church and organization he pastors is centered on restoration and compassion.

It is easy to come to church daily or weekly and be so caught up in being busy that we lose out on the things that matter most. Our Lord Jesus charged us to show concern for each other, and I have come to understand that nothing builds community in a church more than a genuine culture of compassion and love. This is probably our biggest challenge, which is not surprising when we consider the storm Jesus and the disciples had to go through just to get to the other side and minister to this troubled and rejected man. The Gadarenes were not even Jews since the account of this story in the Bible mentions them herding swine. But regardless of this, Jesus still made the dangerous journey to have this encounter. I believe this story was included in the Bible to teach us a lesson about going all out to reach people in need, even when they are not 'one of us.'. Just consider the compassion Jesus demonstrated in this man's case.

It takes some resolve to become a church that sees through the eyes of compassion. But we must go to the other side if we are going to be effective in demonstrating the kind of compassion that affects our communities and transforms men and women into better vessels.

Another lesson I learnt is that you can be close to your pastor and not have a revelation of who he or she is. A possessed man who was "abandoned" by his community had a sharper revelation of who Jesus was than those who had been walking with Him and witnessing his miracles. When the man saw Jesus, he ran to Him and worshiped at his feet. He was troubled yet he worshiped; he was possessed yet he showed reverence with zero familiarity with the anointed One. Sometimes the people we have no regard for or do not appear to have it all together, the most troubled among us, have the highest reverence and respect for the pastor. Those who appear to have it all together and have access to the pastor usually do not appreciate the depth of the anointing they have access to. Before I understood this truth, I used to wonder why my pastor would seemingly give a lot of his time and attention to people I thought did not deserve it. Jesus never came to save and help those who were OK; He came to save and help those who need it.

It is my wish for every church to establish a culture of compassion that reaches everyone. Everyone needs help! People need someone to talk to. Some are crying inside but have to hide it and pretend all is well. The church is made up of people who do not have it all together, but it is in that same church that some feign surprise when they are exposed to the parts of others that are crippled. We must go to the other side!

LESSON 4—DON'T QUIT

Many have asked me how I managed to serve in our church and be attached to my pastor for so long. I know it is quite uncommon to see people stay with their pastor and serve consistently for over 25 years without losing interest or leaving. Though uncommon, why does it have to be strange? We live in a time where commitment and loyalty have become scarce, so people see it as unusual when someone is able to demonstrate those traits and live them out. It ought not be so. My heart yearns to see the days where service and commitment were the pride of the church, when we were just proud to serve and did not know what it meant to quit. We happily served even when the roles we were assigned were not our preferred roles.

I remember being part of a mass choir in school many years ago. I used to play the bass guitar with 11 other bassists! Out of the 12 of us, one was in a class by himself and got to play most of the songs. Most of us played only two songs within a full academic year, yet none of us ever complained or missed rehearsals. We were just happy to be part of the choir. None of us quit or saw our lack of playing a reason to walk away. When I was a music director, I recall a few instances where some of the singers quit because they weren't frontline singers, while others waned in enthusiasm, and, like Peter, began to follow afar off because they were offended by what appeared as preferring others over them.

I have experienced many hard times that could have caused me to quit. When the recession of 2008 hit, I lost most of my investments, enough to make me give up and focus on my life, but I kept serving. I remember having surgery in 2015 while still turning up that same weekend to play piano for worship service because the substitute keyboardist unexpectedly called out at the last minute. I gingerly made my way to church and got on stage to play without anyone but my family and my pastor knowing what I was going through. I just did not know how not to be present and serve when I was needed. I have also endured a lot of hurts and misrepresentations over the many years I have been serving in church, some which cut me deeply and made me cry. Many of these incidents could have justified my decision to quit, but I kept holding on. I knew I had been called to this and I could not just vacate my position and walk away because of a negative situation or because of my displeasure at someone else. I had already made the connection between service and my blessing, so I kept constantly trying to focus on the task I had been assigned regardless of the opposition and trials I faced. Service was the investment I had to protect until I reaped the expected harvest. So I made it my job to keep the external pressure from affecting it.

Be careful of the critics. There are always seats in churches occupied by individuals who have taken on the mantle to criticize everything they suspect, see, and hear. If you do something right, they find a way to criticize. If you do something wrong, you're toast. They forget that those who have rolled up their sleeves to work in the pit are more vulnerable to making mistakes because they expose themselves publicly to the potential of error. The fear and pain of criticism and gossip have stopped many from serving in church. But some of the people serving in our churches have issues that defy their commitment to keep serving. I know one lady who has had almost every negative thing happen to her, and yet she turned up every weekend to serve. Anytime a need to serve was present, she would be one of the first to volunteer. I used to observe her in wonder at how someone like her could be so committed, and I pray in expectation that God will reward her. She had resolved within her that the tongues of men or the disappointments she faced in life would not cause her to break. Serving in church became her hiding place and solace, and she protected her portion as if it were all she had. The more people criticized her, the more she served. She is priceless!

So have this attitude within you always - treat your service in the house of God as though it is all you have left. Be ready to protect it and prevent anyone from causing you to walk away from it because no one is worth giving up on that life investment.

LESSON 5—NEVER JOSTLE FOR POSITIONS

This lesson touches on the importance of keeping our eyes on what we've been assigned without wavering or seeking to maneuver our way into a position of responsibility before we are ready for it. Getting into a position you are not prepared for will end up crushing you. Having been a casual observer of human behavior in church, I have seen this happen multiple times. Some see service as a vehicle to gain relevance or recognition through a position of responsibility, and not a vehicle for the intrinsic benefit of serving others. This is caused by selfish ambition and being interested in nothing but in one's self. The whole premise of serving is totally opposed to all the characteristics of selfish ambition.

Ambition in itself is a good thing. It is usually defined as a strong desire to do or to achieve a goal out of determination or hard work. Selfish ambition, on the other hand, is all about seeking one's interests regardless of how it affects others. Philippians 2:3-4 speaks on selfish ambition and how we ought to live:

> Do nothing from selfish ambition or conceit, but in humility count others more significant than yourselves. Let each of you look not only to his own interests, but also to the interests of others. (Philippians 2:3-4, NKJV)

Paul, one the greatest generals of the Christian faith, wrote this text to admonish the church on the basics of true service—to serve the interests of others as we care about ours. In the same text he warned against doing things in church out of selfish ambition, as it moves us away from serving out of humility and love for others. This even happened among Jesus' disciples during the Last Supper as He was about to face His greatest trial. While they were seated next to Jesus, they started arguing about who would be the greatest. I am still not sure why they picked that time to begin that argument, considering it demonstrates a total lack of understanding of the task at hand. But Luke 22:24 says strife arose among the disciples when they needed to be attentive and focused on their master, Jesus:

> And there was also a strife among them, which of them should be accounted the greatest. (Luke 22:24 KJV)

Selfish ambition will always generate strife. Even the disciples forgot who they were and the season they were in and started bickering about their positions. This is a classic example of people jostling for a position closer to the pastor.

Sometimes people serve because they want their pastor to notice them, so they use their service to gain access to him or her. In their minds, the only motivation and reason for their service is the pastor, not the love for people or their obedience to the scripture we just read. I have learned never to force myself into positions of authority just because I want to be noticed. I might get the position and realize I really didn't want it. For 20 years I made teaching the choir my pride and joy. All I focused on was ensuring the choir never failed to deliver. I was not interested in getting any acknowledgment from my pastor or adulations from men. Whether my pastor was at church or out of the country doing missionary work, my commitment never wavered. His acknowledgment of my efforts and service were not relevant to me. I did not seek to be made a pastor as others came through our ministry and got ordained because I knew that was not my call at the time. All I desired was to be given room to serve and build a choir that was relevant, anointed, and empowered for ministry.

For many of those years, I was not even part of the close team that supported my pastor and engaged in high-level meetings with him. But as I kept being faithful and kept doing well what had been assigned to me, I started getting pulled into meetings with my pastor because of my commitment to the vision. After a while, he appointed me head of the church board to help guide the affairs of the church. Soon he had me training local pastors and those in other cities to set up effective systems that support growth in ministry. All this started happening after many years of developing trust and staying faithful to what had been committed into my hands.

We have already been warned against serving with self-ambition, but there is another warning Proverbs 25 I wanted to bring to your attention:

> "Don't work yourself into the spotlight; don't push your way into the place of prominence. It's better to be pro-moted to a place of honor than face humiliation by being demoted." (Proverbs 25:6-7, MSG)

Assuming I had forced my way into this position without adequate preparation, I would have been unprepared for the many situations that arose, and my failure to deliver effectively would have eventually demoted me from the position I found myself in. This also works in our corporate world. If you try to get into a role you have not been ade-quately prepared for, there is a good chance you will be demoted. Bide your time and be patient.

While in service, be sure to learn the lessons that come your way. There is always something to learn if you incline your ear to hear and your eyes to see. God has crafted a unique position for you. Do not allow selfish ambition to sway your perceptions and cause you to miss out on the opportunities He has available. If you bide your time and stay faithful in the little you have been given, you will be entrusted with much more. So, wherever you find yourself…whatever your hands find to do…do it well as unto God.

LESSON 6 – YOUR SERVICE IS ULTIMATELY TO GOD

Even though in church we serve men, the ultimate recipient of our service is God alone, for Christ said when we serve in church, we are ultimately doing it for ourselves. Think back to the altar of service I mentioned in a previous section. Whatsoever your hands find to do, do it well as unto God. The narrative of the final judgment in Matthew 25 says:

> But when the Son of Man comes in his glory, and all the angels with him, then he will sit upon his glorious throne. All the nations will be gathered in his presence, and he will separate the people as a shepherd separates the sheep from the goats. He will place the sheep at his right hand and the goats at his left.
>
> "Then the King will say to those on his right, 'Come, you who are blessed by my Father, inherit the Kingdom prepared for you from the creation of the world. For I was hungry, and you fed me. I was thirsty, and you gave me a drink. I was a stranger, and you invited me into your home. I was naked, and you gave me clothing. I was sick, and you cared for me. I was in prison, and you visited me.'
>
> "Then these righteous ones will reply, 'Lord, when did we ever see you hungry and feed you? Or thirsty and give you something to drink? Or a stranger and show

you hospitality? Or naked and give you clothing? When did we ever see you sick or in prison and visit you?'

"And the King will say, 'I tell you the truth, when you did it to one of the least of these my brothers and sisters, you were doing it to me!' (Matthew 25:31-40, NLT)

Anytime I read this text, I reflect on how I am serving and living my Christian life. This is why I have tried to be present always and serve even when I do not feel like serving. This is why I have tried to be urgent in season and out of season because I never know who I will encounter on any given day. This is why I seek out opportunities to do good even when it is sometimes inconvenient. I have tried to give to others who were in need even though I knew they would never pay me back. Remember, the scripture says anything we do for others in need, we do for God. This should spur us on to good works. This should cause us to serve always with the end in mind.

This is why we should never allow anyone to make us vacate our positions in the house of God. It is one of the biggest attacks on our destiny and reward. Things will not always be smooth sailing and not everyone will be at peace with us or our service. But that should never provoke us to turn back and vacate our positions. Over the years, I have seen so many people leave the very positions they committed to uphold just because the felt offended by someone. Why would you give up the thing that God has placed in your hands to manage just because someone rubbed you the wrong way?

Why would you leave a church and walk away from the covering of a good pastor just because somebody in the church offended you? As I mentioned earlier, multiple opportunities could have made me walk away if I had not had an understanding of my unwavering commitment to serve regardless of how I felt. But I held on to the truth in Matthew 25. I believed God had called me to do what my pastor had entrusted me with. I understood that my service was to God and should not be subject to the whims of men.

LESSON 7 – EVERYONE IS WEIRD, INCLUDING YOU

I know this sounds funny, but it is true. The church you serve in is a combination of weird people, including you. We are all weird. Everyone we encounter in our communities has developed a unique personality and a way of seeing and doing things. It is what makes them who they are, and the same applies to you. Of course, some are more enlightened than others by virtue of the exposure they have had, but they are still weird. But herein lies our challenge: our ability to merge our different personalities (regardless of our weirdness on the weirdometer scale) and work together effectively to achieve team and organizational goals. That is always going to be difficult especially in a church setting. I have had more success building and leading teams in the corporate world than I have been able to accomplish in church. And that is not to say anything negative but to acknowledge the difference in dynamics between the two settings.

Many people who have contemplated serving in a church or decided to quit after serving only briefly in a department have found the challenge of dealing with others quite daunting and an unnecessary burden in their lives. Many have said "I don't need this" and have walked away or decided to just sit in the pews to enjoy the service organized by those same weird people they decided they could not work with. Carey Nieuwhof makes the following observation:

> Yep. Church is messy, flawed, disappointing, and at times deeply hurtful, largely because people are messy, flawed, disappointing and at times deeply hurtful.

When I served as music director in our church for 20 years, I probably met every kind of personality imaginable. The interesting part is I was probably weirder than all of them. Some members were difficult to work with simply because they did not know how to coexist in a group without being the center of attention. Others just didn't have the right work ethic to study their music parts in order to remain relevant or improve their skills. Still others were super-skilled and knew how to hone their gifts to become dependable in the team. But whatever I had to build with, I dug my heels in and ran with it. I always found a way to manage the personalities to keep us focused on our goals. Some people joined us and decided after a short while they could not deal with the choristers. Yet I would see them the very next weekend enjoying the ministry of this same choir, led by the very same weird people they did not want to work with.

Why do I think this is important? Because if we make ourselves so big that we do not open ourselves up to work with and accommodate others, we will never be able to accomplish our goals or our vision. Everyone is different; so are the gifts that everyone brings to the table. The Bible says we have all been made different and are like the human body. Our bodies consist of different parts, which frankly look weird when we compare them with one another. Your hands look weird when you compare them with your ears or eyes. Yet together, they all keep the body operational.

> How strange a body would be if it had only one part!
> (1 Corinthians 12:19, NLT)

If we were all the same, how would we ever produce anything awesome? As this text says, a body would be strange if it were all one part, one personality, or one skill. Our uniqueness is supposed to be part of the tools we combine and exercise to build ministry. We all use keys: car keys, door keys, cabinet keys, etc. They all have different ridges because they are cut differently and made to unlock a particular door. I like to see everyone as a key, specially cut to open a particular door or provide a unique service. No matter how you are cut, you are designed to be the solution to some particular problem.

When certain individuals approach me to point out the "imperfections" of our church and how we could do things better, I always tell them they are part of the solution for the problem they see. Your eyes will always be attracted to the problem you can help solve. So rather than criticize from the bleachers, get involved and bring your uniqueness, which may be what the church has been waiting on to get to the next level. If you find the church to be unfriendly, be the friendly one. Start loving people. If you think a particular group is ineffective, join that group and use wisdom to influence change. It all starts by taking the first step. Do not decide you don't want to be part of a particular group because you don't need drama in your life. If you do not help, how can you make a difference? You are the key to unlocking a particular door through your service, so do not withhold doing good.

LESSON 8 – ONE DAY YOU WILL NEED YOUR SERVICE ALTAR TO SPEAK FOR YOU

The story of Hezekiah always encourages me when I run into a tough season. His encounter with the prophet Isaiah is recorded in 2 Kings 20:

> About that time Hezekiah became deathly ill, and the prophet Isaiah son of Amoz went to visit him.
> He gave the king this message: "This is what the Lord says: Set your affairs in order, for you are going to die.
> You will not recover from this illness."
> When Hezekiah heard this, he turned his face to the wall and prayed to the Lord, "Remember, O Lord,

how I have always been faithful to you and have served you single-mindedly, always doing what pleases you." Then he broke down and wept bitterly.

But before Isaiah had left the middle courtyard, this message came to him from the Lord: "Go back to Hezekiah, the leader of my people. Tell him, 'This is what the Lord, the God of your ancestor David, says: I have heard your prayer and seen your tears. I will heal you, and three days from now you will get out of bed and go to the Temple of the Lord. I will add fifteen years to your life, and I will rescue you and this city from the king of Assyria. I will defend this city for my own honor and for the sake of my servant David.'" (2 Kings 20:1-6, NLT)

Here was a king the Bible describes as successful, but who received a judgment from the prophet that the end of his days was near. The Bible says he wasted no time to turn his face and plead with God by pointing out his faithfulness in service. So compelling was his case that before the same prophet who brought the bad news could leave the palace, God directed him back to change the judgment. Hezekiah had built such an altar of service and faithfulness before God that when trouble came knocking on his door, he knew to turn to Him with something in his hands that he could negotiate with. This is intriguing. Look at the following scripture as well:

Thus Hezekiah did throughout all Judah, and he did what was good and right and faithful before the Lord his God. And every work that he undertook in the service of the house of God and in accordance with the law and the commandments, seeking his God, he did with all his heart, and prospered. (2 Chronicles 31:20-21, ESV)

The account says "…and every work that he undertook in the service of the house of God, he did with ALL his heart." This was his testimony he took to God to plead his case. Your service builds an altar for you that will be tested by fire. If you build your service altar scrappily and with no heart, you will have nothing to stand on when you need it.

As I shared earlier, I have had my fair share of situations where I had nowhere to turn to but God. Each time, I pointed to my altar of service and asked God to remember me. Let me share one such instance with you. When I got to my senior year in college and began filling out job applications, I indicated that I needed a company that would sponsor my work permit in London. At the time, the rules required that I go back to my home country upon completion of my course. I had a slim chance of any company sponsoring me because the steps the company would have to go through to justify their intended sponsorship were best avoided.

At that time, I had led the choir for 4 years and we had recorded our first album. Plus I was deeply committed to service and to my pastor. But even though I knew the chances of finding a sponsor were slim, I decided to pray and lift my service to God. I believed I had made myself so important to God that He was bound to help me as He promised before my journey in the London church began.

I applied to two engineering firms and was invited to interview. The first interview was uneventful, and I got through it without any indication I was going to get a job. The following week, I visited the other engineering firm I was interested in as one of more than 90 people who showed up that day. When I sat down and they asked me about my status, the HR manager, who happened to be part of the interview team, told them on my behalf that she would initiate the sponsorship process as long as they liked me. She said the company had just decided to start sponsoring successful applicants if needed! Of course, I was the first to get the privilege. Talk about the timing of this corporate decision. Needless to say, I got selected and the rest is history.

As recently as the middle of 2019, I visited my doctor for a check-up after experiencing some discomfort in my abdomen. During the ultra-sound, I could tell something wasn't right just by looking at the changing expression of the technician who was administering the procedure. I later found out a tumor was growing inside me, which was suspected to be cancerous. I was scheduled for immediate surgery so the mass could be removed. While the medical staff worked to get the surgery scheduled, I had to go through multiple tests (MRIs, ultrasounds and blood tests). But I refused to panic and just kept serving. I walked around the church going about my normal duties as one who had nothing on his mind. It was a battle to keep my mind at peace, but I had seen God come through for me so many times that I knew this would also be resolved.

When the doctor informed me about the tumor, I reached out to my pastor, whom the Bible confirms had been given to me as my earthly shepherd. He quietly listened and asked me to come see him at his home that evening. When I got there, he prayed a simple prayer over me and told me I would be fine. I remember feeling his heart as he prayed for me, and that stirred my faith. He asked God to touch me and for the mass to be benign. He then asked me to go home and to remember that "It is well." When I got home, I prayed a simple but heartfelt prayer and asked God to remember three things: my pastor's prayer, my service that I had faithfully given to the church for over 25 years, and the promise God gave me when I started serving under my pastor. They were like three stones of remembrance I had gathered in my heart.

I brought my case to God and negotiated just like Hezekiah had done. I knew three things: that God would honor the prayer of my pastor over me; that God would not forget my labor of love and service in the Kingdom; and lastly, that God would remember His word to me when I committed to join my pastor to build the ministry. I am a firm believer that God would not lie to me or fail me when I need Him. He had given me His promise that if I take care of His work, He would take care of me. I believe Him.

I eventually went for major surgery on Boxing Day of 2019.

Thankfully, the surgery went well, but I had to wait for the results of the pathology tests on the mass they removed from my body. A couple of weeks later, I got a call from my doctor to come review the results. When I got to his office, he said all the tests came back negative for cancer. He said he was surprised at the results, so he ordered the tests rerun. He confirmed there was absolutely no problem and that I was whole. It was just a benign mass, and I didn't even have to come in for periodic checks. I remember how surprised he looked when he told me the results. He was happy but surprised at the results of the tests. Some may have a "logical explanation" for what I went through, but as my pastor has always said, "A man with an experience is never at the mercy of the man with an argument." This situation made me experience once again the power of service and how the altar I build will speak for me in times of need. Like Hezekiah, I turned to God and called to remembrance the service I had given for so many years of my adult life. Once again, He came through for me. This is why I don't allow anyone to move me off center, lose my focus, and walk away from my place in God. Build your altar well and with the right motives. You will need it on 'Memorial Day.'

LESSON 9 – AVOID STRIFE AND UNFORGIVENESS AT ALL COSTS

If there is anything that can stop the progress of any group in its pursuit of vision, it is strife. James 3:16 KJV says, "For where envying and strife is, there is confusion and every evil work." Strife, more than any other vice, has the power to destroy a team and put the brakes on progress. Many times, I have had to take the less popular position of being the "fool" in order to maintain the peace of the group. Many times, I could have retaliated against others for things they had done to me, but that would only have increased strife. Strife is often subtle. Just having negative thoughts or feelings about someone in your team is enough to start bottling up strife in your heart. I have often seen people who did not like each other sing or serve together in the same group.

There is an interesting scripture in Proverbs 17 that I like so much. It says:

> The beginning of strife is like letting out water [as from a small break in a dam; first it trickles and then it gushes]; Therefore abandon the quarrel before it breaks out and tempers explode. (Proverbs 17:14, AMP)

Most of the time, strife starts with something that may appear insignificant, but you log its occurrence in your heart. Anytime you see the person who offended you, it wakes up a negative emotion in your heart until it becomes clear that you dislike the person. I have learned that if you cannot walk away and ignore issues, then find a way to address them before they become a hindrance. Most importantly, train yourself not to be so emotionally reactive to every little thing that blows by you. I have seen too many people walk away from a good church that feeds them because they got upset with someone. I am sure someone has left our church because of me, but I am so not worth it. If, in my immaturity and moments of weakness, I rub you the wrong way or do something foolish out of frustration that upset you, why allow someone like me, who is so unimportant to your future destiny, to convince you to walk away from where God wants you to be? No one is worth your destiny. If God sends you to a church, there is a reason you have to be there. Stay in your place and wait until that assignment is over.

The early church was of one heart and one mind because Jesus' topmost desire for us, as His body, is unity. That is what set the platform for the Holy Spirit to do mighty things through the disciples. God cannot work in an environment where strife and disunity exist. In His final prayer for His disciples, He asked God the Father to make us one just as He and the Father are one, so the world may have a witness. He knew our unity would enable His work to continue in power. That is why the enemy is always targeting our unity in church, because he knows what God can achieve through us if we come together with a shared passion to see nothing except God glorified.

> "Look!" he said. "The people are united, and they all
> speak the same language. After this, nothing they set out
> to do will be impossible for them! (Genesis 11:6, NLT)

Look at the power of unity! If we come together as one, and speak the same language of love and compassion, nothing will be impossible for us to achieve as a body. This is the reason we struggle so much with strife. It is designed to make us weak and lose our traction toward progress.

It is everyone's responsibility to keep strife from coming between us and maintain unity. We all have a choice to make when we are offended. We can choose to let the issue go or we can choose to make a big deal out of it. Of course, certain things are hurtful, like someone betraying you after you helped them in their time of desperate need. But if you choose to hold on to the hurt and become unforgiving, you will continue to suffer, not the one who betrayed you. Why allow someone to take your peace from you while they walk free, most times without even knowing that you are upset? I have seen my pastor make plenty of sacrifices for people who later left the church without a word. Did he allow the occasion to stifle his drive? Not in the least. He just kept going, counting the cost of the call worthy of the crown he will receive.

We have heard often that keeping unforgiveness in your heart is like drinking poison and expecting the other person to die. When you work as part of a team, your unforgiveness prevents the flow of the Spirit of God from working in and through us. If there is one thing I would like you to remember in this book, it is avoid strife and unforgiveness at all costs. Be super watchful over this vice because it will hamper your progress and, spiritually speaking, make you like a hamster on a treadmill.

LESSON 10 – BE A FAITHFUL CUSTODIAN OF THE "PLACE"

God has made us custodians of our local church and expects us not only to serve but to be loyal to our local church and the vision for which it exists. The "place" is our church and it is where we get fed. It is our safe haven where God has chosen to congregate us so we may edify one another while we pursue the purpose He has called us to, both individually and corporately. It is where we get our healing, comfort, and strength when we go through hard times. This is the place to protect, our church. Now when I say "protect our church," I am not referring to the building but to the body of believers, which includes the pastor. We need to recognize the body we have been joined to is critical to our life and purpose. It is vital that we supply to the body the unique talents and gifts God placed inside us just for that purpose.

From the day you sign up to join a church, you become a custodian of the vision with as much responsibility as your neighbor. A custodian is someone who has responsibility over another entity to provide, protect, promote, and to be present for. That means you cannot take part in any kind of behavior or gossip about your pastor, leader, or neighbor. You have a responsibility to protect your pastor and to make his or her job easier. I have gone into a lot of detail about the burden pastors carry. Please do not make their burdens even heavier if things aren't going right in the church. Your pastor is not perfect; he or she is as human as you.

Every organization's success is highly dependent on the loyalty of its members and can only go as far as its constituents do. While it is true that all things rise and fall on leadership, if your people decide not to move, you are stuck. If your people refuse to respond to ideas and plans to support the vision, the organization will be affected. The more committed and loyal members you have, who make up their minds to support the vision, the healthier your organization will be. Whether or not you choose to serve, you are one of the foot soldiers required to work to establish the vision God has given the church through your pastor. So, if you decide not to serve, or if you decide to be unfaithful in your service, you skew the weight of the work onto those who rise to serve. This is why you see the same number of members carrying the load, burnt out, and in need of rest.

Sometimes things just don't work out and it may become necessary for you to leave. I have seen this happen often, and I respect that. Not everyone is joined to you for the duration of your life's journey. But if you have to leave, please do not badmouth the church and tell all manner of denigrating stories to let others know why you left. After getting your healing, teaching, and covering from your church, why would you then turn away and become an enemy? Read the following scripture:

> "And as for you, O My flock, thus says the Lord GOD: 'Behold, I shall judge between sheep and sheep, between rams and goats. Is it too little for you to have eaten up the good pasture, that you must tread down with your feet the residue of your pasture—and to have drunk of the clear waters, that you must foul the residue with your feet?'" (Ezekiel 34:17-18, NKJV)

Why would you, after all the blessing you received in the church, foul the waters you once drank from? What could have upset you so much that you had to become an antagonist of the ministry that fed you, and prevent others from receiving their blessing from it? What you do to your local church you do to the kingdom of God. When you fight the church, you fight God. I have learnt not to even engage in squabbles or say anything negative about my church. I will not dirty the waters that feed me and my family. Neither will I prevent someone else from coming to be blessed by the fountain in my church. Let us be very careful how we treat the church, which is the body of Christ.

No one is bigger than the church, and as much as we are all

important to God, He has many options to keep His church moving in the direction He has set for it. Hold dear every opportunity to serve. Should something happen that necessitates the need for you to move on, please leave well. Be a faithful custodian of the church. Protect it and be loyal to it, because the purpose of the church is much bigger than you can comprehend. Count it a privilege to be part of it and treat it as such.

MY FINAL THOUGHTS

"If a man is called to be a street sweeper, he should sweep streets even as a Michelangelo painted, or Beethoven composed music or Shakespeare wrote poetry. He should sweep streets so well that all the hosts of heaven and earth will pause to say, 'Here lived a great street sweeper who did his job well."

— *Frederick Buechner* —

Many have struggled with the age-old question of what one's purpose is. When I was younger, I used to struggle with it too. How was I supposed to know what God wanted me to do? What was the reason God brought me into this world, using my parents and family as my point of entry? Why did God lead me to my pastor through my friend, Eva, after she persisted in introducing me to him in 1994? Was it just coincidence, or does it have a direct bearing on my purpose? I believe nothing just happens. Your role on a team at church, your location, and the church you attend did not just happen. I am such a believer in the orchestrated moves of God that I am careful to take every opportunity or unfavorable situation that comes my way seriously because each one could be my opportunity to fulfil my destiny. I don't want to get to the end of my life and regret not having given my best to the opportunities and situations that life presented me.

What if the opportunity to serve that my church has given me is the purpose God assigned me and expects me to fulfil fully without wavering in commitment? At the end of my life, what if God asks me to give an account for the way I served that purpose? What if God gave me those talents to serve the church and not just my corporate life? Why does the Bible admonish us to do well whatever our hands find to do?

I have already shared that some people came together to pray for God to move in Charlotte North Carolina, during a planned evangelistic meeting. Little did they know their prayer would convict a young Billy Graham, who became one of the generals of our faith. What if the lady who kept inviting my pastor to church had given up? How would he have ended up at the church where he stood up alone and went for an altar call to give his life to Christ? Look at the ripple effect his obedience to the call has had on multiplied thousands all over the world. That lady prayed him through and invited him. That's all she had to do, but she did it faithfully and didn't stop until she got my pastor to go to church. She finished her assignment.

If you knew that your service to God was part of His big plan, would you change anything? If you understood that somehow you are God's partner on this Earth and He is relying on you to play your role no matter how mundane it may be, would that affect the way you serve? If you knew that someone hearing you sing would unlock his or her will to receive Christ, would you go back to the choir and start being faithful again? If you have sat down and decided not to serve because "it always ends in drama," how sure are you that God has not called you to that church and those people? Yet we sing songs that contain lyrics like, "Send me and I will go, and I give myself away."

Many years ago, during a time of reflection, I wrote what I call my personal creed, which lays out my beliefs about this matter. I would like to leave you with it:

MY CREED

God loves me too much to allow me to go through life without fulfilling my purpose...the reason for my entry into existence.

I am confident that God loves me too much and is very intent on bringing His purpose for me to pass. So somehow as I go through life, though I may not hear a clear instruction on what my divine purpose is...though I may not have a major purpose that touches the whole world like a Billy Graham, a T D Jakes, a Steve Jobs or a Bill Gates, I will still believe that as long as I don't sit idle, I am working every day toward fulfilling my purpose.

And if I get to the end of my life and have not had the "call" to some major earth-impacting purpose, I will believe that I did fulfill my purpose. Maybe that lady I helped who needed someone to give her advice...maybe the time I spent serving my pastor and remaining loyal to him…maybe that money I gave to support that single mum or jobless friend...maybe that time I spent teaching music to others...maybe that song I wrote that had an impact on and strengthened an unknown someone who has a greater purpose than most was part of my purpose.

Maybe my purpose was to meet my wife and have my kids, one of whom may have a greater-than-me purpose. Maybe my little contribution was a necessary building block in some person's life, which was required to help them get to the next stage of their call.

So, at the end of it all, I played a small part in fitting my piece of the puzzle into that person's life, who ended up fulfilling a major purpose. Somehow, I believe that from God's perspective, we are all connected. His purpose is so great that every little thing I do could be a necessary building block toward something greater.

So, this is my faith...that nothing I invest my time or money or other resource in is a waste. Because I am part of this bigger plan of a God whose ways are higher than mine, I will not take for granted any opportunity I get to apply myself to help or serve. I have this confidence that perhaps anything my hands find to do may be going to help someone greater than myself fulfill something greater per God's great plan.

Because of this, I have pledged that whatever my hands find to do, I will do it well because I may never know... it may be my purpose.

Live well, love much, be happy.

May God bless you always.

THE END